HIPPO EATS DWARF!

Alex Boese holds a master's degree in
the History of Science from the University
of California, San Diego. He is the author of
The Museum of Hoaxes and *Elephants on Acid* and
the creator of www.museumofhoaxes.com.
He lives near San Diego.

Also by Alex Boese

THE MUSEUM OF HOAXES

ELEPHANTS ON ACID
and Other Bizarre Experiments

Alex Boese

Hippo Eats Dwarf!

PAN BOOKS

First published 2006 by Harvest, an imprint of Harcourt, Inc., Orlando Florida

First published in Great Britain 2009 by Boxtree, an imprint of Pan Macmillan

This edition published 2010 by Pan Books
an imprint of Pan Macmillan, a division of Macmillan Publishers Limited
Pan Macmillan, 20 New Wharf Road, London N1 9RR
Basingstoke and Oxford
Associated companies throughout the world
www.panmacmillan.com

ISBN 978-0-330-51291-6

9 8 7 6 5 4 3

A CIP catalogue record for this book is available from
the British Library.

Printed and bound by CPI Group (UK) Ltd, Croydon CR0 4YY

Visit **www.panmacmillan.com** to read more about all our books
and to buy them. You will also find features, author interviews and
news of any author events, and you can sign up for e-newsletters
so that you're always first to hear about our new releases.

TO BEVERLEY

CONTENTS

INTRODUCTION

For the past decade versions of the following news clipping have circulated around the world:

> A circus dwarf, nicknamed Od, died recently when he bounced sideways from a trampoline and was swallowed by a yawning hippopotamus waiting to appear in the next act. Vets said Hilda the Hippo's gag reflex caused her to swallow automatically. More than 1000 spectators continued to applaud wildly until they realized the tragic mistake.

This sensational news item has been reported in the Manchester *Evening News*, Thailand's *Pattaya Mail*, and the Sydney *Daily Telegraph*. It resurfaces periodically, kept alive by the Internet (that vast repository of weird information) until it reappears in print again. In one version the circus is located in Austria; in another, northern Thailand. But whenever it's reported, the tale is presented as fact. However, it's almost certainly not.

The author of the tale probably intended it to be a joke, although we don't know who that author was or where the story was first published. Sometimes it's credited to the *Las Vegas Sun*, at other times to *National Lampoon*, but the tale hasn't been found in the archives of either publication. All we can say with certainty is that it was penned at some time before 1994, when it first appeared in a Usenet posting. It then began its career as a recurring 'true' news story, helped by the fact that many people were willing to believe anything they read online.

The hippo-eats-dwarf story is a) bizarre, b) almost certainly fake, and c) masquerading as real. This set of attributes describes many things in the modern world. Silicone butt implants, for instance. Other examples that come to mind include inflatable girlfriends, lip-synching musicians, pre-recorded laugh tracks, Botox masks, unreality TV, and tofu turkeys. We live in a world that's fake and growing faker every day, in increasingly bizarre ways. We live, to coin a phrase, in a hippo-eats-dwarf world.

There are many reasons for this proliferation of the fake. The most basic one is that confronting reality head-on tends to be unpleasant. We avoid this whenever possible. In fact, our brains seem hard-wired to ignore disturbing truths. It's a kind of survival instinct. As Carl Jung said, 'People cannot stand too much reality.' Instead, we surround ourselves with easy-to-swallow fantasies. Second, fakery is an inevitable by-product of mass culture because fake stuff is cheaper and more convenient than the real thing. We can't all afford to decorate our homes with marble and gold, but most of us can afford cheap plastic substitutes. Third, there are many people (advertisers, politicians, TV producers, etc.) who have a vested interest in lying to us for self-promoting reasons. Finally, advances in technology now allow us to embrace fakery in more elaborate and aggressive ways than ever. Combine all these factors, and what you get is the phenomenon of hippo-eats-dwarf fakery.

But more important than why the world is like this, is how to survive in it. Given the preponderance of fake stuff and the fact that reality itself has taken a turn for the weird, telling the difference between the genuine and the fake has become a constant challenge. That's what this book is about. It offers a tour of our hippo-eats-dwarf world and gives advice on how to find your way in an environment in which the line between truth and fiction has completely blurred.

Assembled in the following pages are thousands of examples of the hoaxes, urban legends, spoofs, scams, advertising ploys, political doublespeak, and other forms of bull (or, as the Brits would have it, 'bollocks') that fill the modern world. Later, when you're trying to figure out if a website selling dehydrated water is for real, or if that photo of a 200-pound cat that just arrived in your inbox is genuine, these examples should provide some guidance on which to base your decision.

This book emerged out of the experience of serving for over ten years as the curator of the online Museum of Hoaxes (museumofhoaxes.com). Day after day I scanned the news to offer readers of the site interesting new examples of fakery. After doing this for a while, themes began to emerge. Recurring patterns became evident. What I've attempted in this book is to record some of those themes. The tour of fakery begins with birth, ends with death, and covers just about everything in between – including eBay. It's structured around a series of 'reality rules' that lay out basic principles for navigating the treacherous landscape of reality, and at the end of each chapter you will find 'reality checks', which are a series of questions you can use to test your ability to differentiate the authentic from the bogus.

But enough said. Let's get down to the business of tracking those dwarf-eating hippos!

ONE

Birth

The subject of birth has always offered fertile ground for superstition and fraud. In Roman times, farmers believed mares could become pregnant simply by 'turning east and inhaling the wind from that direction'. In the Middle Ages, doctors counselled that twins were obviously the product of more than one father. We may think we're too sophisticated to believe such things today, but of course we're not. Baby nonsense has simply transformed to match the times.

REALITY RULE 1.1

Just because a woman looks pregnant, it doesn't mean she is.

You meet a pregnant woman. Or rather, you meet a woman who looks and claims to be pregnant. But how do you know she's telling the truth? This can be hard to determine. After all, short of subjecting the woman to a medical exam, what are you going to do? Poke her in the stomach?

This fact – that to the casual observer a genuinely pregnant woman is almost indistinguishable from a woman who's faking it – is what pregnancy hoaxes depend upon for their success. And while such hoaxes are hardly an everyday occurrence, they're common enough to be a recurring theme in the world of deception.

Consider the 2003 case of Erin McGaw. Erin had an air of innocence about her. Her auburn hair and freckles made her look younger than her actual age of seventeen, and she hung out after school with her church group, not with boys. Which is why her classmates at Penn Manor High could scarcely believe she was pregnant. But the evidence of her growing belly seemed to be proof.

Erin's belly expanded for three months, during which time she discovered that it's not easy being a pregnant teenager. Boys told her she looked fat. Girls whispered behind her back that she must have had a one-night stand, and that she didn't even know who the father was. Erin found herself shunned by her peers.

Finally her teacher, Ms Rottmund, sat Erin down and insisted enough was enough. It was time to tell her classmates the truth – which was that Erin was not pregnant. The only thing she was carrying to term was some padding stuffed into a swimsuit beneath her clothes.

Though Erin's methods were deceptive, her motives were well intentioned. She had conceived of the bogus pregnancy as a way of completing a senior-year independent study project. Her plan was to experience how pregnant teenagers are treated and then to report her findings at the school's year-end Festival of Learning. Erin's parents, as well as Ms Rottmund, had approved the project and promised to keep it a secret. Though unconventional, it was certainly more interesting than most senior-year projects.

Of course, teenage girls conducting school projects are not your normal pregnancy fakers. The typical perpetrators are scam artists trying to make a buck, women such as Maya-Anne Mays who agreed to let Robert and Alette Temple of Walnut Creek, California adopt her soon-to-be-born baby. Eager to make her pregnancy as stress-free as possible, the Temples paid Mays's rent, sent her spending money, and showered her with gifts. But as the months passed, their suspicions grew. Why did Mays stubbornly refuse all medical care? Even though she looked pregnant and had tested positive on a pregnancy exam, the Temples began to suspect something was fishy. Finally, they went to the authorities. Sure enough, there was no baby. Mays was scamming them, as well as two other couples. Her heavy-set build made her look pregnant, and a recent miscarriage had allowed her to test positive on a pregnancy exam. The police charged Mays with three felony counts of grand theft.

Fake pregnancy scams happen often enough that adoption centres keep lists of known scammers, including aliases and dates of birth. But in 2006 a Missouri couple managed to put a novel twist on the con.

Sarah Everson claimed she was not only pregnant, but pregnant with sextuplets. And instead of hitting on a single adoptive couple, she tried to con an entire community. She supplied the Associated Press with a photograph of herself lying in bed looking very, very pregnant. Later, stories of the birth of her six children ran in local papers. Kindly strangers who sympathized with the family's tight financial situation created a website to raise money for them. But where were the infants? Sarah explained they were still in intensive care. But at what hospital? When reporters began to ask these questions, they discovered that no local hospital had ever heard of Sarah Everson or her sextuplets. At which point, the entire scheme rapidly unravelled.

It's important to note the difference between a fake pregnancy scam, in which the scammer knows she's not pregnant, and cases in which a woman actually believes she's pregnant, though she's not. The latter condition is known as pseudocyesis, and it is a genuine, though rare, medical disorder. Mary I, Queen of England, aka Bloody Mary, is thought to have suffered from it. Not once, but twice she believed she was pregnant, only to be disappointed.

Occupying a place somewhere between pseudocyesis and scam is the phenomenon of miracle births. Such cases involve infertile women who claim to be carrying a child, having been impregnated by none other than God himself. This happens more often than one might think.

The cult leader Joanna Southcott remains the most famous miracle-birther. In 1814 Southcott announced she would soon give birth to the Son of God. What made this claim particularly remarkable is that she was sixty-five years old at the time. Nine months passed. Her followers feverishly awaited the birth, gathering every day outside her house. But when the due date arrived, there was no baby. Instead, Southcott died a few days later. Doctors who performed an autopsy found no evidence of pregnancy. So was Southcott cynically manipulating her followers or did she really believe she was pregnant? That's impossible to know.

In more recent times, we have witnessed the ongoing saga of Archbishop Gilbert Deya and his 'holy ghost babies'. This self-styled archbishop (he gave himself the title) convinced numerous female followers in Britain that they were impregnated by Jesus. He then whisked them away to Kenya, where they gave birth in a backstreet clinic – even though most of these women were either post-menopausal or infertile. Furthermore, the 'holy ghost babies' developed within their wombs in record-breaking time. Deya helped one fifty-six-year-old lady give birth thirteen times in three years. For those keeping track, that's approximately one baby every three months. But what made the case of Archbishop Deya really bizarre was that real living, screaming, kicking babies did appear at the end of these rapid-fire pregnancies. Where exactly were they coming from?

The Kenyan government had an explanation. It accused Deya of illegal baby trafficking. His method of operation was apparently to acquire infants in the slums of Kenya and then deposit them into the hands of British women. Strangely, the women appeared unaware of any illegality or deception. Their desire to give birth was so strong that they allowed Deya to convince them they were pregnant. A video of one miracle birth shows a semi-conscious woman, clearly unaware of what is happening, being handed a child while 'doctors' cut an umbilical cord that looks suspiciously like a wire.

Deya now faces charges of child trafficking in Kenya, and the Kenyan government is actively seeking his extradition from the United Kingdom. However, this process is still working its way through the courts. As of November 2008, the British High Court ordered his extradition, but Deya still hopes to appeal the case to the European Court of Human Rights, arguing that he would face possible torture if sent to Kenya.

Of course, the phenomenon of miracle births could not exist without a large gullible population ready to believe such things are possible. The world is in no short supply of such people. This was illustrated during the summer of 2004 when newspapers reported that hundreds of Muslims were flocking to a German university clinic to see a woman who had supposedly given birth to Allah's chosen son. The pilgrims' source for this information? A rumour posted on a Turkish Internet site. They had read it online, so it had to be true.

As more pilgrims kept showing up at the clinic, the staff were at first confused, then amused, and finally frightened. Try as they might, they couldn't convince the miracle-seekers that no woman there matched the description of 'the Mother of Allah's Chosen Son'. The arrival of new miracle-seekers was only stemmed when the clinic hired extra security guards to turn them away.

However, there will always be new rumours, and gullible people ready to believe them. That, unfortunately, is the way of the world.

REALITY RULE 1.2

Human women give birth to human babies.

On 27 June 2004, the BBC published a story on its website about an Iranian woman who had given birth to a frog. Details of the case were sketchy, but an Iranian newspaper (the BBC's source) theorized that the woman had picked up a frog larva while swimming in a dirty pool, and that the larva had grown into an adult frog inside her body. No further details ever came to light about the case, and the BBC published no more on the subject, but what it never acknowledged was that these kinds of tales, about women giving birth to non-human creatures, have been around for millennia, and they're as dubious now as they were back then.

Pliny the Elder, writing in the first century AD, described a

Roman woman, Alcippe, who gave birth to an elephant. He also wrote of the birth of a half-man/half-horse creature called the Hippocentaur, which he claimed to have seen preserved in honey. Not to be outdone, the seventeenth-century Danish physician Ole Worm (his real name) displayed two hen's eggs in his museum that supposedly had been laid by a Norwegian woman. The eggs became prized collectors' items. One of them came into the possession of the king of Denmark and was eventually sold at auction in 1824.

Then came the notorious case of Mary Toft. In 1726 this British woman stunned the medical community by claiming to have given birth to rabbits. She even performed this feat while being observed by the king's personal surgeon. Unfortunately for Mary, she tried to perpetrate her scam – the goal of which was to gain a pension from the king – at the dawn of the age of science, and early scientists demanded that such an extraordinary claim be backed up by extraordinary evidence. To this end, the physician Sir Richard Manningham threatened to operate on her to examine her miraculous uterus. Mary quickly confessed.

In addition to these tales, there is a long history of European folk legends that cultural anthropologists refer to as 'bosom serpent' legends. It is these that the BBC's frog-child was a direct descendant of. In such tales, various animals – snakes, spiders, ants, frogs – crawl into a woman's body, grow to full size, and later emerge in horrifying fashion (through the skin, out the mouth, etc.). Anthropologists theorize that such tales represent fears about the dangers of pregnancy. An enduring modern urban legend of this type is the tale of the Octopus Birth, in which an unfortunate girl gives birth to an octopus after getting octopus eggs inside her while swimming. Folklorist David Jacobson documented an instance of this tale reported as news by a Boston newspaper in 1934. Given that the BBC published an almost identical version in 2004 (substituting a frog for an octopus), the legend is evidently still alive and well.

There is a disturbing but sensational sub-genre within the larger corpus of tales of women giving birth to non-human creatures. This is the concept of a human–ape hybrid. From the eleventh century comes the story of an Italian countess who fell in love with her husband's pet ape, mated with it, and gave birth to a half-human/half-ape child she named Maimo. Later, the pet ape grew jealous of the countess's husband and killed him in a fit of rage. Perhaps inspired by this tale, in the 1920s a Soviet biologist, Il'ya Ivanov, actually did experiment with creating a human–ape hybrid. For years, reports of his experiments were dismissed in the West as wild rumour, until the opening of Soviet archives in the 1990s revealed them to be true. Thankfully, all Ivanov's attempts proved unsuccessful, and his career was cut short when he was thrown into a prison camp.

More recently, a captive chimp named Oliver attracted attention because of his eerily human facial structure and forms of behaviour. There was speculation he was a 'humanzee' (human–chimp hybrid), but genetic testing conducted in 1996 revealed he was fully chimp.

It would be nice to dismiss the idea of a human–chimp hybrid as a twisted, pseudo-scientific notion. Unfortunately, the jury is still out on that. Sceptics argue that chimps and humans have a different number of chromosomes. Therefore, a hybrid offspring should not be viable. However, horses and donkeys have different numbers of chromosomes, and they quite readily produce mules when mated together. There are reputable primatologists, such as Geoffrey Bourne, former director of the Yerkes Primate Center, who have speculated that a human–chimp hybrid might indeed be a biological possibility. So while we can classify the stories of women giving birth to frogs, octopuses, rabbits, and snakes as urban legends and hoaxes, the concept of a human–ape hybrid remains more ambiguous. Let's just say that, for now, it appears highly unlikely, and hope we never see the day when this is proven otherwise.

REALITY RULE 1.3

Women give birth to children. Men don't.

When a woman is pregnant, it occasionally happens that the father of the child will experience some of her symptoms. He might develop strange food cravings and feel muscular pains. This phenomenon is known as a sympathetic pregnancy or, more technically, as Couvade syndrome.

Some cultures ritualize this experience, subjecting fathers to various forms of torture and deprivation so they can sympathize with the woman. Nowhere is such a ritual perfected more than among the Huichol Indians from Central Mexico, who lay the father in the roof of the hut above the labouring woman. Whenever she feels pain, she tugs on a rope that is tied around the father's testicles. A less alarming alternative is offered by the Birthways corporation, which manufactures a strap-on 'empathy belly' that allows fathers-to-be to experience the symptoms felt by expectant mothers, including weight gain, shortness of breath, bladder pressure, backaches, fatigue, irritability, and 'much, much more!'

In rare cases, a sympathetic pregnancy might proceed so far that the father's breasts begin to swell and even lactate.

Few men realize they possess all the biological equipment necessary to produce breast milk, but the evolutionary biologist Dr Jared Diamond notes that, for a man to produce breast milk, 'mere repeated mechanical stimulation of the nipples suffices in some cases, since mechanical stimulation is a natural way of releasing hormones'. However, starvation is a far more reliable method since it interferes with the liver's ability to flush out excess hormones. Dr Diamond writes that 'thousands of cases [of spontaneous lactation] were recorded among prisoners of war released from concentration camps after World War II'.

Of course, the easiest way to make a man produce milk is to inject him with female hormones, though eating too much junk food and drinking tap water might have the same effect. Doctors report a sharp rise in the number of men experiencing gynaecomastia (unwanted growth of the mammary glands). They speculate this might be caused by an increasing amount of female hormones in our food supply, coming from farmers who use the hormones on cattle as well as from trace amounts of the female contraceptive pill in our water. If this trend continues, men might end up being like domesticated goats or the wild dayak fruit bat. The male members of this species produce milk relatively often and without any obvious external stimulus.

Could a man go a step beyond sympathetic pregnancy and actually give birth to a child? Rumours of pregnant men have floated around for years. On the web you'll discover an entire subculture that fetishizes the idea. But, to date, there's never been a scientifically documented case of a man 'in the family way'.

Men lack the biological parts to become pregnant like women. Therefore, a man could only bear a child via what is known as an ectopic pregnancy. A surgeon would have to transplant a fertilized egg into the man's abdominal cavity, and then give the man female hormones to encourage blood vessels to grow around and feed the developing egg. This may sound straightforward, but getting it to work in practice would be both difficult and dangerous.

During the 1960s Dr Cecil Jacobson, a researcher at George Washington University Medical School, claimed he had successfully implanted a fertilized egg into a male baboon and allowed the egg to develop for four months before terminating the pregnancy. However, Dr Jacobson never showed the baboon to other scientists and never published his results, so you have to take his word for it that this happened. Since Dr Jacobson was later arrested for secretly impregnating seventy-five patients at his fertility clinic with his own sperm, his word no longer holds much weight in the scientific community.

More recently, the website malepregnancy.com purported to document the first case of a man to bear a child. Although the site looked real, and featured video clips and pictures of the father-with-child, it was in reality an art project dreamed up by conceptual artist Virgil Wong. But in 2002 a Beijing doctor, Chen Huanran, based at the Chinese Academy of Medical Sciences, announced he was recruiting volunteers to participate in a 'male mother' study. He said his goal was to help transsexuals realize their dreams of giving birth. As of his last public announcement, in 2005, he had four volunteers, but there have been no updates since that time.

In America, in early 2008, the dream of a male mother appeared to have at last been realized. At least, that's what headlines proclaimed, and what a widely circulated photo of a man sporting a very large belly and stubble on his chin seemed to support. The reality was more complicated. The man, Thomas Beatie, was a transgendered individual who began life as a female. Thanks to a series of surgical operations and testosterone injections that suppressed her menstrual cycle, she became a he. In other words, Beatie had all the necessary biological parts to become pregnant. It was simply a matter of stopping the testosterone injections and allowing his body's natural hormones to rebalance themselves. To male-mother purists, this wasn't quite the same as an actual male pregnancy. Still, the media loved it and showered him with attention. He even got to appear on *Oprah*.

Although Beatie may not have qualified as the first true male mother, it seems plausible that doctors may someday perfect the techniques to make male pregnancy a reality. At which point, Reality Rule 1.3 will need to be revised.

REALITY RULE 1.4

People will make jokes about anything. Even babies. Even dead babies.

In 1729 Jonathan Swift published a short work titled *A Modest Proposal for Preventing the Children of Poor People in Ireland From Being a Burden to their Parents or the Country, and for Making Them Beneficial to the Public*. In it he suggested that enormous social and economic benefits could be gained by feeding the unwanted babies of the poor to the rich.

Of course, Swift did not actually intend to promote class-based cannibalism. His point was to use satire to dramatize how the rich exploit and dehumanize the poor.

Swift's short work subsequently lent its name to a genre of satirical hoaxing that uses the same method. Such works are called Modest Proposals. The satirist pretends to advocate an idea that people find shocking or disgusting. But the true goal of the satire (at least, according to the satirist) is to raise awareness of a social problem.

If you want to find present-day examples of Modest Proposals, simply go online. It's difficult to spend half an hour browsing the Internet without stumbling across one. But the problem the genre raises is that it's often very difficult (close to impossible) to distinguish between a person who is seriously advocating a disturbing idea and someone who is doing so satirically. After all, there are genuinely twisted individuals out there proposing all kinds of deviant ideas. People inevitably mistake Modest Proposals for the work of genuine sickos, and outrage follows.

For instance, what would you think if you happened upon the Arm the Homeless Charity, which collects donations to provide firearms, ammunition, and firearm safety training for homeless people? A press release issued to the American media in December 1993 announced the formation of this charity, and a national controversy ensued. Critics denounced the charity on all the major networks, and angry letters poured in to newspapers. However, the charity wasn't real. It turned out to be a Modest Proposal dreamed up by a couple of university students who claimed they were trying to raise awareness of violence and gun safety.

What about the website IBuyStrays.com? It purports to represent a business that buys unwanted pets and resells them to research labs. Text on the site encourages animal owners who have grown tired of their pets to sell them in order to help the research industry. Again, it's a Modest Proposal. Its creator claims to be attempting to focus attention on the (legal) trade in research animals.

One final example: ChrissyCaviar.com. This is the website of Chrissy Conant, who sells eggs harvested from her own body, preserved in tubal fluid, as 'human caviar'. She suggests that one day her caviar will 'surpass Beluga caviar as the current ultimate in luxury, consumable items'. Chrissy Caviar, unfortunately, is real. Performance artist Conant actually *has* harvested eggs from her body and does offer them for sale, though technically she sells them as works of art to avoid food safety regulations.

Critics of the Modest Proposal genre argue that, whether or not such works raise awareness of social issues, they're still in poor taste. There's no good answer to this. People's tolerance for this kind of thing varies. The important thing is to recognize that the genre exists, and it's not going away. So if you stumble across something that really turns your stomach, consider whether it's a Modest Proposal before you call the police to have the people arrested.

REALITY RULE 1.5

Be wary of clones lacking proof.

In 1962 John Gurdon, a researcher at Oxford University, announced he had successfully cloned frogs from adult frog cells. Gurdon's announcement generated enormous excitement within both the scientific community and the larger public. Before this time, the idea of cloning an animal had been considered to be the stuff of science fiction. Gurdon's research indicated it was technologically possible. And if a frog could be cloned, why not a human? Scientists weren't willing to say such a step would happen any time soon, but hoaxers were more than ready to suggest this.

In 1978, on the heels of the debut of *The Boys from Brazil*, a movie about the creation of Adolf Hitler clones, respected science journalist David Rorvik startled his peers by announcing the birth of the world's first human clone. Rorvik was vague about the details. He described a top-secret project conducted on a faraway tropical island, funded by an eccentric millionaire codenamed 'Max'. The clone, Max's exact genetic match, couldn't be introduced to the public, Rorvik explained, because of concerns about the child's privacy. Instead, Rorvik asked that everyone simply take his word for it that the clone did exist.

This is a consistent theme in clone hoaxes. The purported clone is explained to be emotionally or physically fragile, and so must be kept off-stage, away from public scrutiny.

Rorvik probably thought he was going to ride his tale of a human clone all the way to riches. His book about the experiment, *In His Image: The Cloning of a Man*, did become a bestseller. Unfortunately for him, one of the scientists whose research he cited sued him for defamation. In a technical ruling the court declared that Rorvik's book was a 'fraud and a hoax' as he failed to reveal his sources, and most of his earnings vanished in legal fees.

Rorvik's hoax turned out to be just a warm-up for the phoney clones that materialized following the 1997 announcement of the birth of Dolly, the world's first cloned sheep. The scientifically verified birth of a cloned mammal gave credence to the idea that a human clone might soon be possible. What resulted was a mad rush to cash in on the publicity that would flow to the first group to produce a human clone.

First at bat was Dr Severino Antinori, an Italian physician who announced in late November 2002 that he had consulted for a consortium of scientists that claimed they were about to produce the world's first. The mysterious consortium of scientists never materialized, nor did the clone. Not to be outdone, the Raelians, a previously obscure alien-worshipping cult, convened a press conference a month later to announce they already had a clone. Delivering the news was Dr Brigitte Boisselier, a woman whose peculiarly bright red hair and manic grin became as celebrated in the media as the clone announcement itself. According to her, scientists at Clonaid, a Raelian-funded biotech company, had helped a client give birth to a healthy girl clone named Eve in late December. *Of course*, the clone had to be kept hidden, to protect the child's privacy.

More Raelian clones followed. By February 2004 there were supposedly seven of them, with seven others on the way. The Raelians also claimed to be building a 'Babytron', an artificial, out-of-body womb in which future clones could be grown. Some day, they promised, we would all be able to grow clones of ourselves in babytrons, download our memories into these clones, and thereby live forever.

Rael, the titular leader of the Raelians, later halfway admitted that all these announcements were a hoax when he remarked, 'Even if you want to think that we did all that only for publicity, it is wonderful. If that is the case, we are promotional geniuses . . . But if what we say we did is true, we are also scientific geniuses. In any case, we are geniuses! Wonderful! In any case, we win!' He was right. The Raelians achieved worldwide notoriety and generated a steep rise in their membership on account of the clone mania.

Completing a clone-hoax trifecta, in 2004 and 2005 the highly regarded South Korean scientist Hwang Woo-Suk published articles in the journal *Science* in which he claimed to have successfully cloned a human embryo – the first time this had ever been achieved. A year later his reputation crumbled when allegations emerged that he had faked his data. At first Hwang denied the allegations, but eventually he acknowledged flaws in the data and apologized for 'creating a shock and a disappointment'. He was later indicted on charges of fraud and embezzlement.

It seems likely scientists will eventually figure out how to clone a human. But in the meantime, researcher Gabriel Weinberg suggests an ingenious way a fake clone could be created that would pass any test the scientific community could throw at it. The method is to fertilize an ova via in-vitro fertilization, then divide the resulting embryo to produce identical twins (perfectly doable with today's technology). Allow one embryo to develop, be born, and grow up, but freeze the other. Eighteen years later, implant the frozen embryo into the womb of the grown-up twin and allow her to give birth to it. The resulting child would be an exact genetic match of her 'mother'. She would be an apparent clone, though in reality just a twin.

If, eighteen years from now, a researcher announces the birth of the first human clone, it will be difficult to know if it is a genuine clone, or merely the creation of someone who decided to take Weinberg's suggestion seriously.

REALITY RULE 1.6

Dolls are not, nor should they be confused with, real human babies.

Throughout the history of human civilization children have played with dolls. In fact, dolls have been found in Egyptian tombs over four thousand years old, making them the oldest

Baby Alive!

known toys. It's perfectly natural for children to play with dolls. However, at some point in the evolution of this toy, doll-makers decided that their creations should not merely represent babies but actually be as close as possible to the real thing. That's when dolls went from being cute to being weirdly creepy.

Kenner's Baby Alive doll, introduced in the early 1970s, might have been the first errant link in this evolutionary chain. The doll ate, drank, and even wet its diapers. Kenner's advertising campaign depicted young girls growing deliriously excited at the sight of Baby Alive eating her food.

The trend advanced a step with the introduction of Cabbage Patch Kids in the late 1970s. These dolls were originally high-quality, hand-sewn cloth creations made by artist Xavier Roberts, but due to their popularity they soon were being mass produced out of vinyl. The dolls didn't look particularly lifelike, but their selling point was that they were not supposed to be treated like dolls. Instead, they were supposed to be considered real babies. And you didn't buy them. You adopted them.

Those considering adoption could watch Mother Cabbage giving birth to the baby at the toy store. Mother Cabbage was essentially a bunch of leaves with a hole from which the baby would emerge. Technicians administered Imagicillan to ease the pain of childbirth. The vinyl child was ceremonially spanked to make sure it was alive, and adopters were then asked to take an oath, 'I promise to love my cabbage patch kid,' before being allowed to carry it home.

The extent to which buyers embraced this fantasy is demonstrated by people such as Maryland residents Pat and Joe Posey, who have cared for a Cabbage Patch Baby for over nineteen years. Kevin, as they've named him, has his own

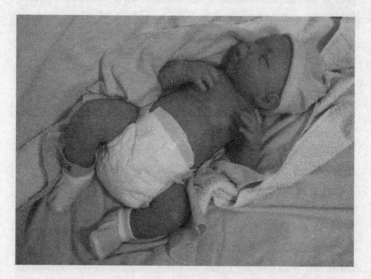

Anatomically correct Little Grace. Sold by Ashton-Drake Galleries.

room in their house – as well as his own college fund, just in case he ever decides to make it on his own. To entertain Kevin, the Poseys take him fishing or let him watch reruns of *SpongeBob SquarePants*, his favourite show. And when company comes over, the Poseys insist Kevin be included in the conversation. Kevin even talks back, though guests are expected to ignore the fact that it's really Mr Posey speaking in falsetto.

Reborn Dolls were the next step in the evolution of human–doll hybrids. Amateur hobbyists, mostly stay-at-home mums, started creating these in the early 2000s and selling them on eBay. Reborn Dolls are ultra-true-to-life, realistic down to such anatomical details as pseudo-umbilical cords.

Quality varies, but to make a really good Reborn Doll you start with a silicone vinyl doll, take it apart, remodel its mouth and nose, replace its hair with human hair, paint it to give it the appearance of a newborn's veiny translucent skin, fill it with sand to get it up to baby weight, add glass eyes, and insert silicone pads to simulate baby fat. Finally you name it and print out a birth certificate. The finished product can be indistinguishable, at first glance, from an actual child. Collectors who sell them on eBay often receive angry emails from people who think they're auctioning off real, human babies.

Collectors pay thousands of dollars for top-quality Reborn Dolls, and true enthusiasts treat their dolls just as they would treat a real human baby. They hug them, pamper them, and dress them in cute baby outfits. They explain that acting in this way somehow fills a void in their lives.

Perhaps the creepiest pseudo-human dolls are those fashioned to resemble specific individuals, particularly when those individuals are dead. For instance, in 2008 Floridians were shocked at the murder of three-year-old Caylee Marie

Anthony, especially when her mother was charged with killing her. But the publicity from the event inspired one company to imagine there might be a market for an 'Inspirational Caylee Sunshine' doll that sang 'You Are My Sunshine' when her belly button was pushed. The company pointed out that it hadn't made the doll to closely resemble the real-life Caylee since that would be 'too morbid and difficult for the public'. Nevertheless, it dropped its plan to sell the doll after receiving a flood of criticism.

The trend towards making dolls appear human definitely makes many people uneasy. This sense of unease has perhaps been responsible for the success of the *Child's Play* horror film franchise, which follows the murderous exploits of Chucky, a Good Guys doll animated by the soul of a serial killer.

The research of Japanese roboticist Masahiro Mori offers some scientific insight into this discomfort. During the 1970s, Mori tested people's responses to anthropomorphic robots. What he discovered was that people easily formed emotional attachments to robots that didn't look human at all. They also bonded with robots that were indistinguishable from humans. But robots that were in between, that were 'almost human', triggered strong negative reactions. People felt a sense of revulsion when they looked at them. Mori referred to this response as the 'uncanny valley'. And what was true with his robots is true with dolls.

Mori suggested that if a robot or doll is obviously not human, then we don't judge it by human standards. This allows us to form an emotional attachment with it. But if the doll looks almost human, we do judge it by human standards, but we simultaneously sense that it's not quite right, which triggers the sense of strangeness.

But what is obvious is that the 'uncanny valley' syndrome

affects people to varying degrees, and some don't seem affected by it at all. Which may be why Baby Alive dolls continue to be popular. They're now marketed by Hasbro, and they've been updated since the 1970s. The newest model is the animatronic Baby Alive Learns to Potty. It eats special 'green beans' that it processes and excretes out the other end, announcing what it's done by declaring, 'I made a stinky!' The doll comes with a warning: 'May stain some surfaces.' Diapers are extra.

Reality Check

Question 1. This photograph shows the outline of a foetus's foot pressing against the inner wall of its mother's stomach. Is it real or doctored?

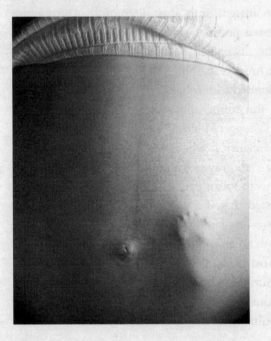

Question 2. TNS Recovery Complex is a brand of face cream made from the foreskins of circumcised infants. True or false?

Question 3. RonsAngels.com was an Internet site that allowed infertile couples to bid for the eggs of supermodels. True or false?

ANSWERS

1. This photograph began circulating online in mid-2004. Its source remains a mystery, making it impossible to say with 100 per cent certainty that the image is fake, though this seems almost definitely to be the case. Although a woman will often see her belly bulge when a baby thrusts out a limb, the abdominal wall is simply too muscular and thick to allow a footprint to be seen with this clarity. The only way a foetal footprint could be seen in this way would be in the rare case of an ectopic pregnancy, which this photo does not appear to show. In addition, the footprint seems disproportionately large for a foetus.

2. TNS Recovery Complex (the TNS stands for Tissue Nutrient Solution) is a real product that does contain ingredients derived from the foreskins of circumcised infants. But if you're imagining foreskins ground up in a blender, that's not the case. Foreskin cells are grown in a medium, and nutrients are siphoned off from this brew. The product was originally developed to help burn victims, but eventually made its way into the beauty market. Reportedly it works quite well.

3. RonsAngels.com debuted in October 1999, and purported to allow couples to bid for eggs from supermodel donors. The *New York Times* thought the site was for real, and published a story warning of a new age of 'commodification' of human egg donation. In reality the site was an elaborate publicity stunt for an online pornography business.

Bodies

Science and technology have brought us closer to realizing an ancient dream: the ability to mend and alter our bodies. But many changes aren't done out of medical necessity. Instead, they're driven by personal vanity. So instead of the *Six Million Dollar Man*'s 'better, stronger, faster', we end up with weirder, freakier, and faker.

Fashion models don't look like that in real life.

Celebrities and fashion models may be naturally good-looking, but they're not quite as good-looking as they appear in magazines where their skin is always flawless, their teeth pearly white, and their hair perfect. They get *a lot* of help.

For instance, make-up and lighting can do wonders for a person's appearance, but that's old school. Nowadays it's often easier to change the photograph than it is to change the person. Thanks to image manipulation software, graphic artists can erase wrinkles, remove blemishes, even out skin tone, melt away fat, enlarge breasts, and shrink tummies, all with the click of a mouse. 'Digital plastic surgery' has become so common that it's rare to find a photo in a fashion or entertainment magazine that hasn't been touched up.

When does touching up go too far? Few people have a problem with removing pimples or stray hairs. In fact, most celebrities demand magazines take care of such details. Eyebrows are only raised, figuratively speaking, when photo editors change people's bodies so much that the photos no longer look like the real life people, and (more importantly) when this is done without permission.

Graphic artists enlarged Kate Beckinsale's breasts so enormously in the poster for her film *Underworld* that it seemed like false advertising. The actress felt obliged to tell them to tone it down a bit. Likewise, Kate Winslet didn't appreciate it when she saw that her picture on the cover of *GQ* had been digitally massaged to make her look leggy and skinny. She was proud of her more rounded real-life appearance, boasting that all the men she knew 'like girls to have an arse on them'. However, Victoria Beckham didn't protest when the poster ad for her new perfume, Intimately Beckham, showed her sporting a full, curvy behind, though sceptics noted that in real life her buttocks appeared much flatter. There was similar frenzied speculation about the authenticity of the frontal bulge David Beckham displayed in a 2007 Armani underwear ad.

The power of photo manipulation isn't limited to digitally flattening stomachs or enlarging breasts. In extreme cases a magazine editor can opt for 'total body replacement' – transplanting a person's head onto someone else's body. This happened to Julia Roberts, much to her displeasure, on the July 2003 cover of *Redbook*. The one mitigating factor was

FrankenOprah

that her head was transplanted onto a younger version of her own body. But the most notorious example of this practice occurred on the 26 August 1989 cover of *TV Guide*, which showed daytime talk-show host Oprah Winfrey lounging in a gauzy dress on top of a pile of money. Oprah looked gorgeous, but only the head belonged to her. The body came from a 1979 publicity shot of Ann-Margret. The composite

BODIES 31

was created without the permission of Oprah or Ann-Margret, and was detected when Ann-Margret's fashion designer recognized the dress.

But what you see in fashion magazines is just the tip of the iceberg. Descend further and you'll soon encounter a vast, murky world of fetish-driven photo manipulation.

Those nude pics of your favourite actress you may find on the Internet? They're probably fake, created by some enthusiast who spent long, sweaty hours on their creation. Far more disturbing are the pictures of ultra-skinny models that the web also plays host to. Usually dressed in bikinis, these wraiths pose cadaver-like, skin clinging to their emaciated frames.

The pictures are the products of the 'pro-ana', or pro-anorexic, community. These unfortunate sufferers of body-image disorder, who feel they're never skinny enough, digitally alter photos of models to make them appear skeletal. The images then serve as 'thinspiration', motivating the pro-ana to starve themselves further.

Confusion arises when the non-pro-ana stumble upon the photos and think they depict real models who have starved themselves down to skin and bones. They don't. Generally speaking, models are not encouraged to be so skinny that their appearance is frightening, though many of them really do need a cheeseburger in a bad way.

REALITY RULE 2.2

No body part is more lied about than the penis.

There may be an entire industry devoted to preying on women's insecurities about their looks, but men have their own hang-ups, particularly in regards to the organ between their legs.

Of all the creatures in the animal kingdom, humans actually do not possess the largest penises in relation to their body size. That honour goes to the barnacle. Mankind comes in second. But man definitely comes in first in the list of 'animals who care most about penis size'. At some point in man's evolution penis size became equated with virility and social dominance. Having a large penis meant you were the alpha male. A modern example that illustrates the enduring fascination with large penises is the curious tale of Rasputin's penis.

In 1916 a gang of Russian nobles drugged and poisoned the mystic Grigori Rasputin, who was believed to be the lover of the Tsarina Alexandra Feodorovna. When that wasn't enough to kill him, they beat him, shot him, and finally drowned him in the Neva River. At some point during this process, they cut off his penis, which was reportedly over thirteen inches long. Once detached from him, it embarked on a strange career of its own.

A cleaning woman is said to have found and preserved it. Subsequently, it came into the possession of a group of Russian women living in Paris who worshipped it as a holy relic, keeping it inside a wooden casket. Rasputin's daughter, Marie, objected to her father's penis consorting with these women and demanded it back. It stayed with her until she died in California in 1977, after which an antique dealer found it tucked away in a velvet pouch along with some of her manuscripts. The dealer sold the by now well-travelled penis to Bonham's auction house, whose experts then discovered, to their surprise, that what they had bought was not a penis, but a sea cucumber.

Everyone assumed the real penis was lost. But in 1994 it, or something purported to be it, resurfaced at the newly opened Russian Museum of Erotica in St Petersburg. Igor Knyazkin, the museum's director, explained that he had acquired it from a French antiquarian, though he offered no explanation of where the antiquarian had obtained it. So was it really Rasputin's long-lost member? Who knows. The controversy continues.

Most men do not have a penis the size of Rasputin's, but that doesn't stop them from pretending they do. The most popular method of artificially boosting the male endowment is simply to lie about its size. This is so widely done that it should be considered the norm among men. Ask a man how large his penis is, and you'll inevitably receive an answer that errs on the plus side. This was one of the accidental discoveries of early scientific efforts to collect data on penis size. The Kinsey Sex Report surveyed men during the 1940s and concluded that the average penis size was 6.3 inches. However the survey left it to the men themselves to do the measuring, assuming they would tell the truth. Apparently, they didn't. More recent studies, in which less trust was placed in the participants, have all come up with lower numbers. For instance, in 2001, Lifestyles Condoms set up a tent outside a nightclub in Cancun, Mexico and had nurses measure the penile dimensions of hundreds of college-age guys. The average measurement was 5.87 inches. In other words, either the men in the 1940s were exaggerating, or in a mere sixty years the average penis size shrank by .43 inches.

A more visual form of endowment-enhancement is to display a prominent bulge in one's trousers. For years men have achieved this using socks, salamis or other appropriately shaped objects. In a memorable scene from the rock parody

This Is Spinal Tap, a band member tries to pass through airport security with an aluminium-wrapped cucumber shoved down his pants. But men need no longer rely on such low-tech forms of deception. Lee Cooper offers a line of Packit Jeans styled to maximize 'trouser frontage'. And if you don't want to wear jeans, then any pair of pants can be made to appear suitably stuffed, thanks to a polyvinyl insert named The Bulge. The Bulge, its manufacturer informs us, 'keeps its shape twenty-four hours a day and can be cleaned in a washing machine'.

Pseudo inches are not enough for some men. They want real growth. Scam artists take advantage of this desire by hawking a wide variety of penis-enhancing products, often via email, including pills, creams, pumps, and sprays. There are even companies that promise results via hypnosis. (*'Imagine your penis. It is growing larger . . . larger.'*) The fact that there is no scientific proof any of these products work doesn't stop men from spending hundreds of millions of dollars on them every year.

An option for the more adventurous is to tie weights around the penis and stretch it. Proponents of this method point to the Karamojong people of north-eastern Uganda as evidence that it works. For ritualistic reasons, Karamojong boys reportedly attach weights to their penises at puberty. After years of doing this, they succeed in stretching their phalluses to lengths of up to eighteen inches. However, there is little scholarly documentation of this practice – except for a few eyebrow-raising pictures, such as one that shows a Karamojong warrior with a penis so long that he must tie it in a knot to keep it out of the way when not in use.

As an interesting side note, there does exist a small sub-culture of penile weight-lifting enthusiasts. A martial art known as Jiu Jiu Shen Gong is devoted to this practice. The world record holder is a man in Hong Kong who claims he can lift a 165-pound barbell with his penis for ten seconds.

Finally, some men turn to surgery for enlargement. Unfortunately for them, the penis doesn't respond well to surgical augmentation. One method is to sever the ligaments that hold the penis upright so that it hangs further out from the body. This does make the penis appear longer, but also prevents it from standing upright when erect. Another technique, disturbing but true, is to inject the penis with fat cells culled from cadavers. None of these methods is guaranteed to produce permanent results. In fact, things can easily go disastrously wrong. Many men who go this route end up with grotesquely deformed penises shorter than they were before. A cruel twist of fate, if ever there was one.

REALITY RULE 2.3

If it doesn't look natural, then it probably isn't.

For over a hundred years surgeons have sought to alter, and hopefully improve, the shape of the body. Demonstrating society's priorities, much of this effort has focused on making women's breasts larger. Early breast augmentation techniques were crude and dangerous. Doctors experimented with implanting paraffin, goat's milk, fat cells, glass balls, and plastic sponges before they hit upon silicone.

According to legend, silicone was first used for breast augmentation after World War II, when Japanese prostitutes injected it in liquid form in an effort to make themselves more desirable to American GIs. Liquid silicone worked, temporarily, but it also led to discoloration, open sores, and even gangrene, which is why it's now illegal. Finally, in 1961, Dr Thomas Cronin and Dr Frank Gerow developed the silicone breast implant: a hard, elastic sac filled with gooey silicone gel. It was an overnight success.

Women do not always augment their breasts to make themselves appear more attractive. Sometimes financial gain is the motive. Rumours spread in the early 1990s that cartels were smuggling drugs by implanting them into women's breasts and buttocks. In 1994 a woman travelling from Bogota to the US was actually caught doing this. Her unusually large buttocks were what tipped off police.

And then there are cases of women motivated by more obscure emotional reasons. Take, for instance, Sandi Canesco of Australia who injected her husband's ashes into her breast implants after he died in a car crash. She was quoted as saying, 'It dawned on me that if I carried Dustin's cremated remains in my breast implants, I'd never really have to part with him at all.'

Most surgeons have now switched from silicone to saline implants due to concerns about the health effects of silicone leaking into the body, but there is another, highly controversial technique known that involves 'silly string'. In the late 1990s the Houston surgeon Dr Gerald W. Johnson (the man responsible for the late Anna Nicole Smith's cup size) began implanting polypropylene string into women's breasts. This substance absorbs fluid from the body and expands after implantation. Women with these implants saw their breasts grow larger and larger indefinitely, swelling to massive proportions. This caused serious complications, which is why regulatory agencies quickly banned string implants, but for a short time they were seized upon by performers in the adult entertainment industry who were vying for the title of biggest-busted woman in the world. Incidentally, the top contenders for this title boast measurements of around 42XXX. At that size they're so top-heavy they have difficulty balancing on their feet.

Whatever the method used, breast augmentation remains one of the most popular surgical procedures in the world. Hundreds of thousands of women get their breasts enlarged every year. There are even reports of teenagers asking their parents for implants as birthday presents.

For women unwilling to go under the knife, there are alternatives, though most are varieties of quackery. Diane de Poitiers, mistress of King Henri II of France, tried to enlarge her breasts by washing them with a mixture of sow's milk and gold. The mistress of King Charles VII, on the other hand, used a blend of poppy water, ivy, rose oil, and camphor. For modern women, there are options such as Bust-up Chewing Gum or F-Cup Breast Enhancement Cookies, both of which promise 'larger, fuller, firmer breasts' due to the chemicals they contain that mimic the female hormone oestrogen. There are even breast-enlarging ringtones for mobile phones that will 'increase the breast measurements of those who listen to it'. How is unclear. The ad copy states that 'it's a technique involving subliminal effects'.

In 2003 Thai officials launched an initiative encouraging women to perform daily exercises to enlarge their breasts – rather than pursue potentially risky augmentation surgery. The Health Ministry kicked off the bust-boosting operation on a street in Bangkok by lining up a group of women who proceeded to massage and squeeze their breasts (while wearing T-shirts). As might be expected, this demonstration attracted quite a crowd. Whether the campaign achieved any measurable results in terms of bra size has yet to be seen.

There is one non-surgical product that might actually work: the Brava Vacuum Bra. Debuted in 2001, this product clamps over the breasts, forming a vacuum seal. Tests indicate that if a woman wears this device for at least ten hours a day, for a couple of months, she might increase her breasts by a cup size. The downside: it's almost as expensive as surgery, delivers far less dramatic results, and (of course) requires a woman to wear powerful suction cups stuck to her chest.

Breasts are not the only body part to be shaped and augmented. Calves, pecs, biceps, triceps, and buttocks can all be surgically enhanced. Some day we may all have perfect bodies without ever going to the gym, thanks to gel-filled sacs beneath our skin. Even feet can be redesigned. Surgeons report that women, with increasing frequency, are asking for operations that allow them to slip into their favourite high heels and get that all-important 'toe cleavage'. Options include shortening toes to allow feet to squeeze into pointed shoes, and injecting collagen into the balls of the feet to make it easier to walk in high heels. Such operations can result in crippling injuries, but for some people no risk is too large for the sake of fashion.

If you don't think you need any plastic surgery, some surgeons might disagree. For instance, perhaps you suffer from 'batwing disorder' or 'violin deformity'. These are unpleasant-sounding names the plastic surgery profession has invented to describe body shapes that are actually perfectly normal and healthy. The only thing wrong with them is that they deviate from the Hollywood ideal of beauty. Batwing disorder, for instance, refers to the loose skin many women develop under their arms as they grow older. Violin deformity describes wide hips. Then there's hypomastia (the medical problem of having small breasts), or ptosis (saggy breasts).

Finally, not even animals are safe from the plastic surgeon's knife. The CTI Corporation has developed plastic testicles, marketed as 'Neuticles', to replace the testicles lost when a male pet is neutered. Supposedly the prosthetic testicles help the pet maintain its sense of masculinity. The CTI in the company's name stands for Canine Testicular Implant.

In 2003 there was scandal at the prestigious Crufts dog show when Danny, the three-year-old Pekinese who walked away with Best in Show, was rumoured to have had a snout lift. Danny was cleared of all charges and his good name restored, but the controversy demonstrated that the age of the canine nip-and-tuck is upon us. Braces, dye jobs, hair extensions, and even tattoos along the inner eyelid (to add definition) are all strategies owners can use to make their dog look his best for the big show.

Even cows are being beautified. At the 2004 Royal Queensland Agricultural Show in Australia four people were disqualified after suspicions of 'udder tampering' were raised. This heinous crime involved injecting substances into cow udders to make them grow larger. Evidently with cows, just as with humans, a little augmentation can make a big difference.

REALITY RULE 2.4

No one in Hollywood has their original body parts.

Hollywood lives on gossip, and one of the best things to gossip about is what's been done to whose body. Did Michael Douglas have a facelift? Did Mickey Rourke try Botox injections? Did Angelina Jolie have cheek implants? The questions go on and on, but sometimes the rumours go from merely catty to truly bizarre. In the weirdest cases, they even turn out to be true.

For instance, in 1988 actress Barbara Hershey had collagen injected into her lips. Nowadays that would be no big deal, but back then it was big news and inspired a copycat craze in Hollywood. But Hershey's appearance also inspired a rumour that one day, while she was flying in an airplane, the pressure in the cabin caused the collagen in her lips to expand and explode. The rumour was a variant of an urban legend about a woman who wears an inflatable bra onto an airplane and is forced to go to the bathroom, red-faced with embarrassment, to deflate herself after the cabin pressure causes the air in her bra to expand. In reality cabin pressure will cause neither collagen lips nor inflatable bras to expand.

When Cher's celebrity was at its peak she was plagued by a rumour that she had her lower ribs removed to make her waist thinner. A 1988 *Paris Match* article reported the rib-surgery rumour as if it were a fact. It wasn't. Cher sued *Paris Match* and won. She even hired a physician to examine her and certify he couldn't find any evidence of rib-removal. But Cher does admit she's had work done on her nose and breasts. She also points out that she exercises a lot to stay skinny.

The tale of Lara Flynn-Boyle and her sphincter is one of the more bizarre celebrity rumours out there. According to the rumour, which made its way into gossip columns in early 2003, Lara Flynn-Boyle opted for the ultimate vanity procedure: she had her sphincter bleached. Why anyone would want or need to have this done is not clear. Fortunately possible complications were said to be few except, of course, the risk of lifelong anal leakage. This inspired celebrity columnist

Simon Doonan to comment, 'Wax and pluck if you must, but don't tinker with your sphincter.'

But when it comes to celebrity surgery rumours, no one outdoes Michael Jackson. His claim to the title of King of Pop may be in jeopardy, but his reign as the King of Awful Plastic Surgery will forever be secure.

It's said that, at various times throughout his career, he has taken female hormones, had eyeliner tattooed around his eyes, had an artificial cleft added to his chin, had cheek implants, bleached the skin on his entire body (including his genitals), and had pubic hair transplanted onto his jaw to allow him to grow a goatee. It's also said that he uses red lipstick, dyes his eyebrows, wears a wig, and covers his body in powdery white make-up. All of which pales in comparison to the rumours about his nose.

As early as 1981 it was evident Jackson had done something to his nose. It looked dramatically thinner, although still good. By the 1990s it no longer looked good. It had become a small, triangular pointy thing out of place on his face. Its appearance fuelled rumours that he had undergone multiple nasal surgeries.

The rumours reached a crescendo on 13 November 2002, when Jackson appeared in Santa Maria Superior Court to defend himself against charges relating to a contractual dispute. He showed up wearing a surgical mask, which the judge promptly ordered him to remove. Jackson did so, revealing a large bandage on his nose. This sight immediately breathed new life into an old rumour alleging that the tip of Jackson's nose had collapsed or fallen off because of the extensive surgery performed on it, forcing him to wear a prosthesis. Without the tip he supposedly resembled 'a mummy with two nostril holes' (as *Vanity Fair* columnist Maureen Orth

Michael Jackson in Santa Maria Superior Court.

put it). The bandage, according to the rumour, was holding the tip on.

We shall let Jackson have the final word, as it is, after all, his face. Jackson has vehemently denied all the rumours. In a 2003 interview with Martin Bashir he insisted he had never had plastic surgery, except for two operations on his nose to allow him to breathe better and sing higher notes. He attributed the dramatic whitening of his skin to a medical condition known as vitiligo. The altered shape of his face, he explained, was simply due to the natural ageing process.

Reality Check

Question 1. In 2002 the World Health Organization predicted that the gene for blond hair will become extinct within the next two hundred years. True or false?

Question 2. Plastic surgeon Dr Jonas Zizlesse has pioneered a treatment for obesity that involves transplanting nipples onto fat rolls, arguing that 'fat is only ugly until you put a nipple on it'. True or false?

Question 3. Surgeons in Holland have developed a method to implant small pieces of jewellery into people's eyeballs. True or false?

ANSWERS

1. In September 2002 CBS, CNN, the BBC, and other news agencies throughout the world did report that researchers at the World Health Organization had predicted that within two hundred years there would be no natural blonds left. The gene for blondness would apparently go extinct, driven out of existence by the far greater percentage of dark-haired people in the world. But a week later the WHO issued a press release denying it had said such a thing. Blame for the false story was traced back to a two-year-old article in a German women's magazine that had attributed the 'disappearing blond gene' story to a 'WHO anthropologist' (who didn't exist). A German news agency had got wind of this story and reprinted it. From there it quickly spread around the world. When queried, geneticists said the blond gene is very unlikely to disappear any time soon.

2. There's a certain twisted logic to Dr Zizlesse's argument. As he says, 'Breasts are fat with nipples!' And our society

fixates on breasts, to the point that people pay thousands of dollars to make them bigger. So why not transform fat rolls into pseudo-breasts by transplanting nipples onto them? Nice idea, but it's not real. Nor is Dr Zizlesse. He and his eccentric operation are creations of HyperDiscordia, a satirical online purveyor of 'ontological waste products'. Dr Zizlesse's web page, in which he expounds on the benefits of nipple addition surgery, is one of the many tongue-firmly-in-cheek sites you'll encounter as you surf the Internet (see Chapter Six).

3. True. An eyeball jewellery implant was developed by the Netherlands Institute for Innovative Ocular Surgery in 2002. They call it the 'JewelEye'. Surgeons first anaesthetize the eye with eye drops; then they make a small incision and insert a wafer-thin piece of jewellery beneath the eye's mucous membrane. The implants come in a number of standard shapes (stars, hearts, half-moons, four-leafed clovers, musical notes), but you can special order any design you want. The entire procedure is over in about fifteen minutes, and the implant doesn't interfere with vision or the ability to move the eye in any way.

THREE

Romance

When wooing a female, a male dance fly often brings her a present. Bugs and other food are particularly favoured. But researchers have discovered that the male will sometimes bring a fake gift, such as a seed tuft or a twig. The female will be fooled by the fake just long enough for the male to copulate with her. As it is with dance flies, so it is with humans. Romance and deception go hand-in-hand. Psychologists estimate that dating couples lie to each other during one out of every three interactions. Honesty levels improve among married couples, except that – and here's the catch – the lies they do tell tend to be really, really big ones.

REALITY RULE 3.1

Everyone lies on the first date.

According to sociologists, people constantly engage in a process of 'impression management'. Like actors on a stage, they try to control how others perceive them by selectively presenting information and behaviour that will cast them in the best light. This is a slightly cynical way of saying that most of us try to make a good impression on others. The problem arises when people attempt to create an impression that bears little or no relationship to who they actually are. This happens nowhere more often than in the world of romance.

For many people nowadays, the first impression they gain of a potential romantic partner comes via a personal ad, and it should surprise no one that these ads are notorious for zealously abandoning the principle of truth-in-advertising. Responding to one is a bit like rolling the dice. You never know what you're going to get. For instance, William Coday's ad posted online in 2002 sounded compelling:

> I'm a compassionate, 6'2", 200 lbs., athletic guy who enjoys Mediterranean food, the poetry of Keats and Kavafy, and baroque music. I'd like to get to know you and share interests, experiences and whatever else destiny permits.

What he failed to mention was that he was in jail awaiting sentencing for bludgeoning two of his ex-girlfriends to death. Similarly deceived were the hundreds of men who responded to this ad that circulated online in 2003:

> SINGLE BLACK FEMALE seeks male companionship, ethnicity unimportant. I'm a very good-looking girl who LOVES to play. I love long walks in the woods, riding in your pickup truck, hunting, camping and fishing trips, cozy winter nights lying by the fire. Candlelight dinners will have me eating out of your hand. Rub me the right way and watch me respond. I'll be at the front door when you get home from work, wearing only what nature gave me. Kiss me and I'm yours. Call and ask for Daisy.

Respondents found themselves connected to the Atlanta Humane Society. Daisy was a black labrador. (The ad was the work of an anonymous prankster, not the Humane Society.)

Many personal ads don't represent real people (or dogs) at all. Con artists spam online dating sites with thousands of fake ads as a way to lure men onto porn sites. Many con artists even steal pictures of women who have placed real ads in order to add a veneer of authenticity to their phoney pitches. And dating sites sometimes find themselves having to explain why their ads are not what they appear. The banner ads for JDate, an Israeli dating service, displayed ads that had supposedly run on their site. One included a picture of blonde-haired, twenty-two-year-old Hila from Tel Aviv who was 'looking for a single Jewish guy'. Another showed twenty-six-year-old Sharon who was in search of a husband. In reality the woman described as Hila was Hungarian porn star Kari Gold, and Sharon was Devon Sweet, a bisexual model from the United States. JDate had obtained their pictures from an image archive without realizing their true identities. Any guys hoping to meet Hila or Sharon (or Kari or Devon) via JDate were out of luck.

As an antidote to the less-than-honest norm in personal ads, some Romeos adopt the opposite tack. They go for brutal honesty. This phenomenon was popularized when the *London Review of Books* began running personals and one of its very first ads read: '67-year-old disaffiliated flaneur, jacked-up on Viagra and looking for a contortionist trumpeter'. Brutal honesty immediately became the hallmark of *LRB* personals (leave it to intellectuals to find ironic wit sexier than looks or money), and the trend soon spread to other publications. Of course, it's not always easy to tell when a person is being genuinely honest, and when they're simply trying to be funny.

Esquire magazine, in which this ad ran, swore it was real, but you be the judge:

I am a thirty-year-old virgin on the verge of giving up on love. When I do have a job, it's low paying, and credit consolidators take half of what I earn. I'm behind on my rent, emotionally closed, and take medication to treat my depression. I'm short, not that attractive, a little fat, and have a very small penis. I also have a problem with excessive farting. I studied mathematics in college but still live under the delusional hope of becoming an actor.

Other examples of brutally honest personals include:

Some chances are once in a lifetime. Not this one, I've been in the last 12 issues. Either I strike gold this time or I become a lesbian. Man, 43. (*London Review of Books*)

Ginger-haired Galway man, a trouble-maker, gets slit-eyed and shirty after a few scoops, seeks attractive, wealthy lady for bail purposes, maybe more. (Attributed to the *Dublin News*.)

Bad tempered, foul-mouthed old bastard, living in a damp cottage in the arse end of Roscommon, seeks attractive 21-year-old blonde lady, with a lovely chest. (*Dublin News*, see above.)

Optimistic Mayo man, 35, seeks a blonde 20-year-old double-jointed supermodel, who owns her own brewery, and has an open-minded twin sister. (*Dublin News*)

In contrast to personal ads, face-to-face interactions, such as occur in nightclubs, have the advantage that you can see the physical package you're getting. But people still find ways to deceive. 'Fake fagging' describes the strategy in which a heterosexual man pretends to be gay in order to pick up women. First he gains the woman's trust and friendship, and then he flatters her vanity by claiming her beauty has converted him to heterosexuality.

A New York-based company, WingWomen.com, rents out female friends, or 'wing women', in order to help men pick up women. The service adheres to the 'Domino Theory', according to which, 'Women are attracted to men who have women around them more so then men who have other men around them.' In other women's eyes, the wing woman's presence is a seal of approval (i.e. he's got one female friend, so there must be something OK about him). Soon, the company promises, women will come flocking. It's unclear what happens when these women find out the guy had to rent his one female friend.

One Florida man came up with a novel ploy to attract the attention of women. He pretended to be choking. Women would rush over to help, and once he had 'recovered' he would passionately hug them while declaring, 'Thank you, you saved my life!' The hugging would continue for a long time. His scheme might have been foolproof if in early 2003 a local paper hadn't run a small feature describing how a female restaurant patron had come to the aid of an anonymous choking man. Other women immediately began writing in, noting they had assisted a man of the same description. But the man got away with it because the police concluded he hadn't technically committed a crime.

For every action there is an equal and opposite reaction. And so, while some dream up ways to attract partners, others invent ways to repel them.

The classic low-tech 'leave me alone' excuse is the fake engagement ring. A woman wears a big rock on her finger, to be used whenever a sweaty, middle-aged businessman leans over on the subway and whispers in her ear, 'Has anyone ever told you you're beautiful?' She smiles, shows him the ring, and says, 'Yes. My fiancé. All the time.'

But the fake engagement (or wedding) ring solution isn't perfect. It may send the wrong signal to someone the wearer actually wants to attract. A more targeted option is the Rejection Hotline. Say you're at a club and some guy won't leave you alone. You want to tell him to take a hike, but you don't think he'd listen. What to do? Give him your number . . . though not your real number. Give him the Rejection Hotline number. When he calls it later he hears this recorded message:

> The person who gave you this number obviously did not want you to have their real number. Maybe you're just not this person's type . . . This could mean short, fat, ugly, dumb, annoying, arrogant or just a general loser. Maybe you suffer from bad breath, body odour or even both. Maybe you just give off that creepy, overbearing, psycho-stalker vibe. Maybe the idea of going out with you just seems as appealing as playing leapfrog with unicorns.

Google to see if there is a Rejection Hotline number near you! Email equivalents also exist.

But what if you're already on a date when you realize you can't stand the other person? As long as you have a mobile phone, there's a solution. In 2004 American phone provider Cingular Wireless debuted Escape-a-Date. This service allows a person to prearrange a phone call to interrupt a date, providing them with a graceful exit strategy, should it be necessary. When they answer the call, a recorded message informs them of an attention-demanding emergency such as,

'My friend is having some trouble with superglue and needs help.' The person who uses this technology to flee a date may feel a twinge of guilt later, but it is far more tactful than excusing herself to go to the bathroom and never coming back.

REALITY RULE 3.2

Imaginary friends have none of the character flaws of real friends.

A 2004 survey asked British gamers whether they would prefer to go on a date with Lara Croft, the animated star of the *Tomb Raider* games, or the buxom, flesh-and-blood model Jordan. Sixty-one per cent chose Lara Croft. To many members of the media, this indicated a need for gamers to get out more and experience reality – though it is debatable how 'real' Jordan (being the stage name and persona for Katie Price) is. Nevertheless, the survey did indicate that in today's increasingly virtual world, imaginary friends are becoming both more socially acceptable and more common. In fact, for many they are the love interest of choice.

Judy, a real-life twenty-two-year-old Texas college student, capitalized on this trend by debuting the world's first imaginary-girlfriend dating service. In 2003 she posted an auction on eBay promising to become the highest bidder's 'imaginary' girlfriend. Specifically, the buyer would receive from her a few faux sweetheart letters and emails. She described it as the perfect service for someone who wanted to convince his friends he had a girlfriend in order to get them off his back, who wanted to make an ex-girlfriend jealous, or who figured that an imaginary girlfriend was better than no girlfriend at all.

Judy was overwhelmed by the amount of interest her

service generated. She was flooded with offers, and hundreds of copycat auctions popped up overnight. The average rate was $50 a month, which bought a couple of letters. For those unwilling to spend that much, $14.99 bought a box of chocolates from an imaginary admirer. The truly cheap could opt for an 'imaginary stalker ex-boyfriend'. Only $4.99.

By early 2004 the imaginary-friend business had grown so popular that a company was launched entirely devoted to it: ImaginaryGirlfriend.com. Its website promised, 'You can soon receive personalized love letters by mail, e-mail, photos, special gifts, even phone messages or online chat from your new Imaginary Girlfriend. We won't tell anyone that it's not real!' The best part was that at the end of the contract period your imaginary girlfriend would write a letter 'begging you to take her back'. You could choose to dump her or continue the relationship.

As might be expected, imaginary girlfriends came with no guarantees of authenticity, and in a rather postmodern twist, fake imaginary girlfriends infiltrated the market. One imaginary eBay girlfriend turned out to be a guy named Brian operating out of a car dealership in Omaha.

For the more technologically minded, it is possible to purchase virtual imaginary girlfriends. A Japanese company, Artificial Life, Inc., offers a 'virtual girlfriend' option for mobile phones. A subscriber downloads software that displays an animated girlfriend on the phone's screen. This girlfriend will stop speaking if she's ignored. The only way to win her affection back is to give her presents such as virtual flowers and virtual diamonds, which have to be purchased at extra cost from Artificial Life. She can become very expensive quite rapidly. In this sense she closely resembles a real girlfriend.

'Adrian', the imaginary wallpaper friend.

For those who desire a little more than letters and phone messages, who want the feeling of being with someone, though perhaps not the mess and aggravation of being with someone real, there are other options. Berlin-based interior architects Susanne Schmidt and Andrea Baum sell 'Singles Wallpaper'. These wall decorations are life-sized images of people in various casual poses, such as sitting on a couch or sipping wine. If you glance at them, you'd swear they were real. Schmidt claims their presence 'creates the feeling that there are other people in the room and alleviates feelings of loneliness'. She also notes that in many ways the wall figures are better than real friends because they 'promise to be there all the time and don't leave dirty dishes or argue over the TV remote control'.

To add sound to the imaginary-friend experience, the lonely single can purchase the Amazing Instant Mate CD for only $6.99. Pop it into your disc-player when you arrive home and you'll hear the voice of a pseudo-lover cooing, 'Hello, honey. How was your day? I'm so glad you're home with me. The house is clean, dinner is ready.' As you walk around your apartment, the pleasantries continue: 'You're the greatest thing that ever happened to me'; 'Do you want a foot massage?' The CD comes in both male and female versions.

It is even possible to add a tactile element to an imaginary friend. For instance, you can cuddle up with the Boyfriend Arm Pillow, sold by the Japanese manufacturer Kameo. It's a pillow with a cloth arm attached, designed for women who

PHOTO COURTESY OF ARMPILLOW.COM

The Boyfriend Arm Pillow.

don't want to sleep with a real man but who would like to have an arm wrapped around them at night. Sales have been brisk. Kameo claims, 'Women of all ages have been queuing round the block to take one home.' For men, a rival manufacturer has introduced the Girlfriend Lap Pillow, which is a 'pillow imitating a woman's legs made from urethane foam'. It allows businessmen to nap, pretending they're resting their heads on their girlfriend's lap.

Researchers at Carnegie Mellon have added a high-tech flourish to imaginary-friend pillow technology. They've developed the Hug, a robotic pillow meant for long-distance cuddling. A child can hug her pillow in Kansas and a signal transmitted over the phone lines instructs a partner pillow in Florida to squeeze Grandma. It's meant to bring the sense of touch back to long-distance communication. If a generation of children grows up thinking Grandma is a padded mechanical device, that's an unfortunate but entirely unintended side effect.

And, of course, for the more adventurous, inflatable love dolls have long been available. The Real Doll, marketed by Abyss Creations, occupies the high end of this market. These are anatomically correct silicone-rubber love dolls. Each one is custom made to order and boasts 'ultra-flesh like feel'. The website of Abyss Creations states, 'If you've ever dreamed of creating your ideal woman, then you have come to the right place.'

But if for years all your companions have been imaginary, a day of reckoning might come. You might fall in love with a real person who will ask to meet your friends. Confessing your imaginary life could be awkward. An alternative, if you live in Japan, is to hire the services of a Benriya-san, or 'convenience agency'. These firms provide actors to play your friends. They're often employed at weddings and funerals because in Japan's image-conscious society it's considered shameful not to have numerous people in attendance at these occasions. Very often the groom will never know that half the bride's friends are hired hands.

There is a way to tell the difference between Benriya-san actors and the genuine thing. For a little extra money the actors will also clean your house and mow your lawn. That, of course, is something most real friends would never do.

REALITY RULE 3.3

Whether you score depends on how you keep score.[1]

People have always misbehaved sexually, and they've always dreamed up excuses to explain away what they've done. But there are excuses, and then there are *excuses*.

History records the 1637 case of a French woman who became pregnant during her husband's four years abroad. When pressed for an explanation, she insisted the child had been conceived in a dream featuring her husband. The case came before the Grenoble parliament, who ruled that her husband was indeed the father. This is perhaps the only example of government-certified long-distance insemination-by-dream. Though there was a similar case in the nineteenth century, in which a pregnant woman offered the excuse, 'It's true that my husband has been gone a long time, but we write each other . . .'

---

1. Gene Weingarten, 'Life According To Clinton', *Washington Post*, 17 Sept. 1998.

In recent history, no sexual excuse-maker has been more famous than former President Bill Clinton. When President Clinton was asked during a deposition in the Paula Jones sexual harassment case whether he had ever had sexual relations with Monica Lewinsky, he answered no. When later challenged to defend this answer in light of contradictory evidence, he explained that the court had defined sexual relations as: 'When the person knowingly engages in or causes contact with the genitalia, anus, groin, breast, inner thigh or buttocks of any person with an intent to arouse or gratify the sexual desire of any person.' Based on a careful reading of this definition, he concluded he had not engaged in sexual relations with Ms Lewinsky. His body had touched only her lips – a body part not on the court's list. Of course, her lips had made contact with his genitalia, so she had engaged in sexual relations with him – but not vice versa.

However, President Clinton also had to explain why Monica Lewinsky claimed not to have had sex with him if, by the court's definition, she had. He reasoned that it was her genuine belief she had not: 'I believe if she believed the definition of sex was two people having intercourse, then this is accurate. I believe this is the definition most Americans would give it.' In other words, oral sex isn't real sex. Clinton may have been on firmer ground here. A 1999 Kinsey Institute Poll of 600 college students found that 60 per cent of them agreed with this definition of sex.

But Clinton had one final hurdle to overcome. During the Paula Jones case his lawyer had declared that there 'is absolutely no sex of any kind' between his client and Lewinsky. How could this statement be explained away? Simple. Clinton stated: 'It depends on what the meaning of the word "is" is . . . in the present tense, that is an accurate statement.'

In other words, Clinton wasn't having sex with Lewinsky at the moment his lawyer made that statement. Therefore, the statement was true. What could be clearer?

Honourable mention in the Best Excuses of All Time category must also go to Aylar Dianati Lie, an appropriately named finalist in the Miss Norway competition. Her beauty-pageant career was threatened by allegations she had starred in X-rated films, but she had an explanation. She admitted the woman in the films looked exactly like her, but, she revealed, that woman was her twin sister. Unfortunately for Aylar, investigators checked her story. They found no evidence she had a twin.

No situation is beyond the ability of a skilled prevaricator to wiggle their way out of. Even if you're caught *in flagrante delicto* – you're right there, doing it, and you can't deny it – there is a medical excuse that could come to your aid: sleep sex.

In 2004 an Australian researcher described the case of a middle-aged woman who was sneaking out of her house, finding strangers, and having sex with them. Her partner became aware of what was going on when he found used condoms littering the house. When he caught her in the act one night, she claimed she hadn't known what she was doing because she was asleep. The couple went to see a doctor, who backed up her story – diagnosing her as a somnambulist sexaholic. Sufferers from this condition actually perform complex actions, such as having sex with strangers, while completely asleep.

The problem with this condition is that even if you really do have it – and there's a doctor who's willing to back you up – very few people are going to believe you. You're probably better off with the 'it was my twin' excuse.

Sex and fantasy go hand-in-hand.

There are few more intriguing mysteries in the world than the sex lives of other people. We always want to know more about this subject, particularly about the sex lives of our partners (how do they really feel about us? Are they being faithful?). However, accurate information proves elusive because this is one subject about which everyone lies.

Both genders are guilty in this regard. Men tend to exaggerate their sexual histories, while women minimize them. However, a 2003 study in the *Journal of Sex Research* concluded that women tend to stretch the truth more often than men. The researchers suggested that while men and women have the same libido, women feel more pressure to conform to sex-role expectations, leading them to pretend to be more innocent than they really are.

Women also feel pressure to flatter men's vanity in bed. The result is the Great Fake Orgasm Mystery. A widely quoted study conducted in 2000 by Queendom.com, which surveyed over 15,000 people, found that 70 per cent of women admit to having faked an orgasm at least once in their life.

It is not just female humans who practise this form of deception. Female trout do it too. During spawning the female trout burrows down into gravel and starts to quiver as a sign she's ready to mate. A male then swims alongside her and starts quivering also. If all goes well, their mutual quivering results in the release of eggs and sperm. But if the female senses the male isn't correctly positioned beside her, she'll quiver without releasing any eggs. The male, not realizing she's aborted the process, will go on quivering until he's done. As Erik Petersson of Sweden's National Board of Fisheries said in an interview with CBC Radio, 'The male . . . He's a little bit tricked there.'

Men like to think they can tell when a woman is faking an orgasm, but as Meg Ryan demonstrated in the classic scene from *When Harry Met Sally* in which she faked an orgasm while sitting in a diner, they can't. However, science now can. Neuroanatomist Gert Holstege of the University of Groningen has discovered that positron emission tomography (PET) scanners can sense the changes that take place in the brain during sexual climax, making the machines foolproof fake orgasm detectors. When a woman orgasms, the periaqueductal grey matter area of her brain becomes very active. Not so when she fakes it. However, since most couples don't have ready access to PET scanners, this knowledge won't be of much use to suspicious men.

Women may not need to worry (or may not care) about men faking orgasms, but nowadays they might wonder whether the man's anatomical response is as enthusiastic as it seems. Or has the man received help from an erectile-dysfunction drug such as Viagra? This question prompted the American Association of Retired People to publish rules of Viagra Etiquette. The basic guideline is that a man should inform his date if he's using the drug, but he shouldn't swallow the pill in front of her.

On a broader social level, the mystery of other people's sex lives is the driving force behind a recurring series of panics, most of which involve adults worrying themselves sick about the kinds of behaviour young people might be getting up to. (Of course, when they were kids, no one did anything like that!)

In 2003 school administrators in a Florida high school

banned students from wearing coloured jelly bracelets because they had heard that the bracelets indicated what sexual favours the girls wearing them were willing to perform. Blue supposedly meant oral, black was 'with a condom', red was 'no condom', etc. A national controversy ensued, but subsequent research, including a survey of 300 teenagers by the marketing firm Teenage Research Unlimited, found no high-school students who were aware of the sexual meaning of the bracelets, except in an anecdotal way.

In the same year, a guest on *The Oprah Winfrey Show* raised the alarm about 'rainbow parties'. These were supposedly the new fad in American high schools: oral-sex parties in which each girl came wearing a different shade of lipstick, and each guy tried to leave wearing every colour. As with the jelly-bracelet rumour, all the evidence for these parties came from third-hand accounts reported by adults.

The next year, the British media got worked up about 'toothing'. The story was that young people were using Bluetooth-equipped mobile phones to find sexual partners in public places. The media learned of this practice when a toothing forum appeared online. But a year later the creator of the forum admitted he had intended it as a joke. To his knowledge, no one had ever 'toothed'.

It would be nice to offer worried parents a rule to help them identify false sex rumours. Unfortunately, such a rule is impossible because for every fake sex tale, there's a bizarre sex story that turns out to be true. In fact, sex hoaxes have a way of becoming self-fulfiling prophecies. Broadcast an idea through the media, and eventually someone will take it upon themselves to do it. So while once upon a time no one toothed, or used jelly bracelets to advertise sexual favours, there's a good chance someone now has.

Fake marriage is when you don't really know your spouse. Real marriage is when you know your spouse all too well.

What is a real marriage? In America, thousands of gay couples have been seeking the right to marry, prompting social conservatives to insist that 'real' marriage can only be between a man and a woman. There's even talk of a constitutional amendment that would restrict marriage to different-sex couples.

But if gender requirements were to be formalized in the law, why not go further? Why not make it a legal requirement that marriage is only real if couples love each other?

For some, there already is such a requirement. Every year immigration officials interview thousands of married couples to determine whether their love is real, or whether the two are merely pretending to be in love in order to secure a green card or permanent visa. True love is demonstrated by how well the couples know each other. In other words, the immigration bureaucracy doesn't believe in love at first sight.

Then there's the opposite problem: trying to prove a marriage isn't real.

Luisa Holden insisted that despite the fact that one hundred guests watched her marry Clive Cardozo in an idyllic waterfront setting in Westhampton Beach, she never really married him. The ceremony, she said, was a sham performed for the benefit of Cardozo's sick mother. The marriage licence was never filed, so she thought the whole thing shouldn't count. Unfortunately for Holden, the judge didn't agree. He ruled that 'if it walks like a duck and quacks like a duck and looks like a duck, it is a duck'.

Even better was the reasoning of Dallas-based lawyer Brian Loncar. He defended himself against charges of bigamy by arguing that his second marriage wasn't valid because it was performed by an Elvis impersonator in Las Vegas. The indictment was eventually dropped because of lack of jurisdiction.

If you can't get the marriage annulled, and your spouse is being disagreeable about the terms of divorce, a strategy of last resort remains: divorce a fake spouse. This was the novel tactic employed by an Osaka man who showed up at the divorce court accompanied by a woman pretending to be his wife. Together they participated in the mediation process, filed all the necessary paperwork, and walked out as single people. Or so the guy thought. The one flaw in his plan was that eventually his real wife was sent the divorce papers. She immediately demanded a retrial on the grounds that she hadn't been present during the proceedings. The Osaka court staff confessed it had never occurred to them that they should ask for photo ID at a divorce case.

Reality Check

Question 1. An online dating service, Philanderers.com, caters to married people who want to have extramarital affairs. True or false?

Question 2. A Ukrainian inventor devised a condom that plays music while in use, the volume growing as the wearer's movement increases in intensity. True or false?

Question 3. A North Carolina State University breast cancer study found that women who perform the act of fellatio one to two times a week may reduce their risk of breast cancer by up to 40 per cent. True or false?

Question 4. A Las Vegas company offered 'Bambi Hunts' that involved customers tracking down naked women in the Nevada desert and shooting them with paintball guns. True or false?

Question 5. CheatingScum.com is a website that allows people to publicly expose 'cheating scum' boyfriends, girl-friends, wives and husbands. True or false?

Question 6. A mobile phone accessory is available that projects a high-intensity electromagnetic 'sound cone', inaudible to human ears, but fatal to sperm cells. It serves as an effective means of birth control when placed nearby during moments of intimacy. True or false?

Question 7. Dog condoms, available in three sizes to fit different breeds, are marketed as a way to control canine overpopulation. True or false?

Question 8. An experimental hormone spray, currently being researched, can be sprayed on a woman's forearm once a day like a perfume, eliminating the need for contraceptive pills or patches. True or false?

ANSWERS

1. The number one rule of Philanderers.com is: 'Tell no one, not even your best friend'; and yes, it's real. Toronto-based Doug Mitchell (not his real name) was a married man who enjoyed having affairs. When he realized the web didn't offer many services to facilitate his habit, he set to work correcting that by creating a web-based dating service for philanderers. As of 2002, he claimed the site earned over $10,000 a year, mostly from the sale of personal ads. Men pay $40 for three months. Women advertise for free. His wife, he claims, knows nothing about his side business. Philanderers.com isn't the only site for cheaters. The Ashley Madison Agency also caters to 'attached women seeking romantic affairs and the men who want to fulfil them'. It boasts 160,000 registered members.

2. Reports of musical condoms hailing from former Soviet-bloc countries twice made the papers in the past decade, but appear to have been planted by practical jokers. In 1996 London newspapers reported that a Hungarian, Ferenc Kovacs, had invented a condom that played tunes as it was being 'unfurled'. The default melody was the communist hymn, 'Arise, Ye Worker'. (One reporter remarked that there should also be a Milli Vanilli tune for women who liked to fake it.) But curious travellers who subsequently tried to track down the shop in Budapest where Kovacs sold these singing condoms could never find him. Nine years later, in February 2005, British papers reported a similar story featuring a Ukrainian man, Dr Grigorii Chausovskii. His condom supposedly had 'tiny sensors connected to a mini electronic device that produces the sounds', and played different tunes at changing volume depending on the wearer's position. Chausovskii assured potential users that 'there is no danger of being electrocuted'. But as with the 1996 report, evidence of Dr Chausovskii and his wonderful invention was nowhere to be found.

3. The reason that the NCSU study seems tailor-made for male fantasies is because it sprang from the fantasies of NCSU student Brandon Williamson. In October 2003 he

created a fake CNN webpage reporting this fictitious research study and posted his creation on NCSU's server as a joke. To his surprise, when he returned from the autumn break a week later, word of his site had spread across the Internet and millions of people had visited it. Williamson had loaded the story with clues that it was fake. For instance, he named one researcher Dr Inserta Shafteer. But thousands of people fell for it anyway. Mary Ann Liebert, the publisher of the *Journal of Women's Health*, demanded in a press release that CNN 'investigate thoroughly its decision-making process that allowed a story that is so damaging and degrading to be put up on its website'. She had failed to notice that the story wasn't hosted on CNN's site, which was the biggest clue of all that the article was fake.

4. False. In July 2003 a Las Vegas TV station ran a story about a local company selling 'Bambi Hunts', and an international media frenzy ensued. Only after the media had stewed on the story for a week did it dawn on them that there wasn't any evidence the company had ever conducted Bambi hunts. The company was not currently accepting customers (it said there was too much negative publicity), and everyone who claimed to have participated in previous hunts was highly unreliable. Further research revealed that the company was only licensed to sell videos. If it had run commercial paintball games, it had done so illegally. When the Las Vegas authorities threatened to bring charges against the company, its president, Michael Burdick, admitted no real Bambi hunts had taken place. The story about the hunts had just been a 'hook' to boost sales of a soft-porn video about a fictional Bambi hunt.

5. False. CheatingScum.com debuted in early 2001, promising it would allow people to expose 'cheating rats'. A press

release announcing its launch was sent to the British media, and the site soon got thousands of hits. Visitors could read exposés of rats, and point the finger at scum they knew by posting pictures and rap sheets on the site. However, none of the exposés were real. They were all written by the staff of *.net* magazine, who had created the site as an experiment in viral marketing to see how many visitors they could attract without spending advertising money. But many people thought it was a good idea for a real site, and *.net* received numerous submissions. For legal reasons, none of these were posted.

6. False. David Benjamin wrote a satirical article that he posted online, claiming that the Belgian company Prophy-Lectric had debuted the Nippit 3000 mobile-phone birth-control accessory at the 2004 3GSM World Congress in Cannes. According to Benjamin, the accessory was more effective than condoms at preventing unwanted pregnancy, unless the phone happened to receive an incoming call at the 'moment of truth', in which case all bets were off. The first phone maker with which Prophy-Lectric hoped to partner was, naturally, the German corporation Siemens. Quite a few blogs fell for Benjamin's hoax and reported mobile-phone birth control as a fact.

7. Dog overpopulation is a serious problem. Doggy condoms, however, are not a serious solution. A dog condom vendor appeared online in 2005, offering not only pro-portionally sized condoms, but also lubricated and meat-scented varieties 'to enhance pleasure for both dog partners'. If such a device were real, it would present a number of problems. For instance, both fitting and removal of the protective sheaths would require human intervention. Stopping Fido from eating the latex treat would also be a challenge. In fact, the site was a hoax created by an online condom retailer.

8. True. Tests of a contraceptive hormone spray began in Australia in 2004. The spray delivers a measured dose of the progestin Nestorone through the skin into the blood. If the tests are successful, a commercial version of the spray is expected to reach markets within a few years.

FOUR

Food

In 1957 the BBC news show *Panorama* informed its viewers of the success of that year's spaghetti crop in Switzerland. Footage showed Swiss peasants happily harvesting pasta from spaghetti trees. Hundreds of people subsequently phoned the BBC to ask how to grow their own spaghetti trees. The BBC's deadpan response: 'Place a sprig of spaghetti in a tin of tomato sauce, and hope for the best.' The broadcast was an April Fool's Day joke (arguably the most famous joke in the history of April foolery), but on another level it demonstrated the ambiguous relationship people in the modern world have with their food. We pick up our groceries pre-packaged in supermarkets, usually never knowing exactly what's in them or where they came from. For all we know, our spaghetti *could* have grown on a tree.

REALITY RULE 4.1

Real food rots.

In the 2004 documentary *Super Size Me* filmmaker Morgan Spurlock conducted an experiment with McDonald's food.

He placed menu items such as the Big Mac, Filet-o-Fish, Quarter Pounder with Cheese, and French Fries in glass jars. Then he allowed the food to sit undisturbed to observe how it would decompose. Returning ten weeks later, he found the sandwiches covered, as they should be, in carpets of mould. The fries, however, looked as if they'd just been bought. Not a speck of mould was on them. They were perfectly preserved, like Egyptian mummies.

Real food should rot. The fact that so many of the edibles available in supermarkets and fast-food chains seem to have the miraculous ability to resist the passage of time makes one wonder exactly what they're made out of. Toxic chemicals? Plastic? Widespread rumours suggest that many popular foods are, in fact, made out of indestructible artificial ingredients. What follows are actual claims circulated on the Internet about some of the more suspect foods:

Claim: 'In the 1970s McDonald's used a non-milk shake, and used to use styrofoam balls as a filler (they pass right through you), but they stopped after people who didn't drink their shakes right away and examined the left-over goop realized it and complained like crazy.'

The reality is that McDonald's has never used styrofoam in its shakes. This tale may have been inspired by the fact that McDonald's creates its milkshakes from a powdered mix, rather than from ice cream. Many people claim they can feel the gritty powder of the mix in their throats.

Claim: 'Margarine is but ONE MOLECULE away from being PLASTIC . . . YOU can try this yourself: purchase a tub of margarine and leave it in your garage or shaded area. Within a couple of days you will note a couple of things: no flies, not even those pesky fruit flies, will go near it. (That should tell you something.)'

Spreading margarine all over yourself on a hot day would not serve as an effective bug repellent. But the more important point is that margarine is in no way related to plastic. Margarine is hydrogenated vegetable oil (hydrogenation being the process of bonding a hydrogen atom to the carbon atoms in the vegetable oil). It might indeed be 'one molecule away from plastic', but scientifically speaking, that's a meaningless statement. One molecule can make a huge difference in nature. By the same logic, all the fats in your body might be one molecule away from plastic.

Claim: 'Twinkies (the iconic American sponge finger) are made entirely out of artificial ingredients, and contain no food products. Therefore, Twinkies have a very long shelf life (possibly decades). At some point many years ago Hostess over-produced Twinkies by the billions (possibly due to an error in market research), and could not sell all their stock. So Hostess stored the billions of excess Twinkies in a giant warehouse and waited for their distributors to place orders. However, the distributors did not place orders as large as expected, and Hostess was forced to continue storing the Twinkies. Because of the lack of food products in Twinkies, they do not go bad for a very long time, and to this day the Twinkies that you buy in the store are from the original stock.'

Twinkies are the American brand name for a 'golden sponge cake with creamy filling' made by Hostess. Popular rumour has long held that these cakes are virtually indestructible, although Hostess insists they're just flour, eggs, vegetable oil, and stabilizing agents and have a shelf life of only twenty-five days. The company also denies the secret-Twinkie-warehouse theory, pointing out that seventeen bakeries crank out five hundred million of the treats every year.

Claim: 'Not only is Velveeta clear before food colouring is added . . . its composition is also very similar to that of plastic explosives.'

Velveeta is another American delicacy. (There's a saying over here: 'Twinkies have a half-life, but Velveeta is eternal.') It's a type of yellow-coloured cheese sold in large rectangular foil-covered blocks, which is probably why it might be confused with plastic explosives, although it is actually non-combustible.

Whether Velveeta is clear before food colouring is added is a little more complicated. It plausibly could be. If you examine the labels on cheeses, you'll notice some of them are described as 'processed', while others are called 'imitation'. A processed cheese is a blend of cheeses to which ingredients such as water, salt, artificial colouring, and stabilizing agents have been added. An imitation cheese is made out of vegetable oil and therefore is translucent before the addition of food colouring. Velveeta is a processed cheese. So at no point in its creation should it have been a clear liquid. However, the exact nature of its creation is a secret known only to its manufacturer, Kraft.

On a side note, Velveeta has made its way into the American language. People use the word to describe the process of taking an original item (such as cheese) and creating a more easily consumable but less nourishing version of it. Bibliophiles sometimes complain that Hollywood has 'velveetafied' their favourite books. Used in this sense, the yellow foodstuff could serve as a symbol for modernity itself, as in, 'Mass-market culture has velveetafied reality.'

You never know what you're eating unless you grow it yourself.

In 2003 McDonald's debuted a line of healthier alternatives: a McVeggie burger on a 'toasted whole-wheat bun with barbecue sauce, tomatoes, onions and pickles' and a Whole Wheat Chicken McGrill sandwich. But in a *Chicago Tribune* article, Rosemary Deahl, owner of the Heartwise Express restaurant, pointed out that the nutritional information for these offerings revealed that the bun wasn't actually whole wheat. It was predominantly enriched white flour with caramel colouring.

There's a similar disconnect between many food labels and the foods they supposedly describe. For instance, a consumer might assume there's butter in Blast-o-Butter popcorn, or blueberries in Hungry Jack Blueberry Pancakes, but they would be wrong. If you examine the packaging you'll discover that the blue things in the pancakes are pieces of dextrose, and the popcorn is flavoured with soya bean oil.

What makes this artifice possible is the food industry's not-so-secret secret: artificial flavouring. Thanks to artificial flavours, food scientists can make a piece of cardboard taste like a juicy steak if they want to. So instead of selling us real blueberries in our pancakes they sell us cheap oil-based substitutes flavoured like blueberries. The same goes for thousands of other food products. Manufacturers use the word 'flavoured' on labels as code for, 'This product was created in a lab – nothing in it is real.'

Food manufacturers like to differentiate between natural and artificial flavours, but as Eric Schlosser points out in *Fast Food Nation*, the distinction is dubious. Chemically speaking, natural and artificial flavours are identical. The difference is that 'natural' flavours are produced by using solvents to extract flavour-causing chemicals from food. 'Artificial' flavours are mixed from scratch in a lab. But they're both produced in industrial settings far removed from anything most consumers would think was natural.

The use of blueberry-flavoured dextrose chunks might be misleading, but at least if you read the label you can find out what you're buying. In many other instances food producers aren't as forthcoming. They promise one thing but deliver a cheaper and entirely different substitute, without ever providing the smallest clue about what they've done. The practice is illegal, but widespread.

For instance, do you think that high-priced bottled water you just bought really came from a mountain spring? Think again. In 2003 consumers hit Poland Spring Water, distributed by Nestlé, with a class-action lawsuit alleging the company's marketing claims were deceptive. The original Poland Spring in the Maine woods hadn't flowed since 1967, and what was sold as spring water 'found deep in the woods of Maine' was, according to the suit, actually treated ground water. A year later Coca-Cola had to admit its Dasani brand of bottled water was also nothing more than purified tap water.

The sellers of bottled water look like saints compared to their colleagues in the meat industry. Regulators in the UK recently became concerned when they detected beef and pork proteins in samples of imported chicken nuggets. Unscrupulous manufacturers were buying cheap chicken meat and 'bulking it up' by injecting it with water and the ground-up skin and bones of old cows and pigs. In some cases consumers were lucky if their chicken nuggets were 10 per cent chicken meat.

Ordering fish at bargain seafood restaurants is a similar gamble. When food critic Robb Walsh toured Houston-area restaurants he found all kinds of cheap fish species creatively renamed and offered to diners as more expensive varieties. Pacific rockfish, red rock cod, South African hake, and Gulf sheepshead were all served to him as 'snapper'. He also found lobster tacos that didn't contain lobster but did contain South American langoustine (a kind of large shrimp).

What you get when you buy other meats can be just as surprising. Restaurant chefs often substitute cheap pork for veal, because most diners can't taste the difference. A supermarket in Canada was fined $80,000 for selling 'beef' that was really horse meat. Regulators suspected the store had been making this switch for years. And in Israel authorities seized 80,000 cans that were labelled 'Pâté de foie gras' but contained Bulgarian dog food.

Speaking of dog food, pet lovers might want to think twice about what they're feeding their companions, especially if they're feeding them the really cheap stuff. *San Francisco Chronicle* journalist Keith Wood has exposed some of the most unsavoury practices of the pet food industry. He's witnessed meat renderers grinding up all kinds of unappetizing things – including cats and dogs from the pound – that they then sell to pet-food producers. He even documented cases in which dogs were thrown into the rendering machines with their flea-collars still on, joining the skunks, rats, and raccoons already in there.

Wading further into the nightmarish underbelly of the food industry, we arrive at the Chinese soy-sauce factory that was exposed in 2004 for cutting costs by making its sauce not out of soya beans, but out of human hair. Apparently hair is rich in proteins, just as soya beans are, so if you process the hair correctly it will yield a protein stew that can serve as the base for soy sauce. Consumers were warned to watch out for cut-rate sauces with the word 'blended' on their labels.

If you're not a fan of soy sauce, don't think you're safe. A long-standing rumour alleges that L-cysteine, a common ingredient in a variety of bakery products such as bagels, croissants, and pizza dough, is also often produced from human hair. L-cysteine is typically made out of feathers, hooves, and horns, but there's no reason it couldn't be derived from human hair. If the price is right, who's to say that some unscrupulous manufacturers might not be throwing barber-shop clippings into the mix. To paraphrase the immortal words of Charlton Heston in *Soylent Green* (a 1973 movie about a dystopian future in which society survives by canni-balizing its dead), 'Soylent Bread is PEOPLE. IT'S PEOPLE!!'

REALITY RULE 4.3

People will eat anything.

Hufu stands for human-flavoured tofu. According to its manufacturer, this vegetarian delicacy 'simulates the texture and flavour of human flesh'. Meatshakes, on the other hand, are the eponymous product of the MeatShake chain of fast-food restaurants. They're milkshakes into which ham, beef, or chicken have been blended. And SnackSacks are edible sleeping bags made out of compressed beef and textured protein. They're marketed to backpackers who want to progressively lighten their loads on long hikes by eating what they have to carry.

These three products share one thing in common. They don't exist. They're hoax foods found only on the Internet.

But when it comes to bizarre foods, hoaxers have a hard time outdoing reality, because there is apparently nothing so disgusting or weird that someone, somewhere won't eat it, if they can fit it in their mouth. Consider the following:

1. Turkey Testicles. They may not be everyone's cup of tea, but they're considered a delicacy in the American Midwest, where they're called 'turkey nuts' or 'turkey fries'. Annually for the past twenty-five years the town of Byron, Illinois has hosted the world-famous Turkey Testicle Festival. 'Come and have a ball' is its slogan. Calvin Schwabe, author of *Unmentionable Cuisine*, notes that turkey testicles are the perfect complement to a good martini.

2. Cat-Poop Coffee. Kopi Luwak is not only the most expensive coffee in the world (it retails for about $280 a pound), it's also made from beans excreted by the Indonesian Palm Toddy Cat. Workers must hand-pick the beans out of the cat's faeces, which explains why the stuff is so expensive. It's marketed in America with the slogan 'Good to the last dropping'. (Just to clarify, regular house cats *do not* have the ability to produce this stuff.)

3. Army Worm Wine. Ray Reigstad of Duluth, Minnesota creates this vintage by mashing up army worms (which hang in web-like sacs from trees), adding sugar, water, yeast, and other ingredients, and letting the resulting wicked cocktail ferment. He says the end product tastes like Pinot Grigio or white Bordeaux. Wines of meaty or buggy varieties are also common in Asia. Travellers report finding snake wine and even animal-penis wine in restaurants in China and Vietnam. Reportedly, the more venomous the snake, the better the wine. These wines are created by adding the animal (or animal part) to rice wine – meaning the animal itself isn't part of the fermentation process. Thus, when you order a bottle of snake wine expect to see a big snake staring out of the bottle at you. Ditto for the penis varietals.

4. Tapeworms. Doctors used to sell diet pills that contained tapeworm heads. Once the desired weight loss was achieved, the tapeworm was removed with poison. It should be noted that any doctor who prescribed tapeworms to a patient nowadays would probably get locked up. Tapeworms do consume the food you eat, but they also consume all the necessary vitamins, leaving you malnourished. Plus, you can look forward to your immune system reacting to the presence of a large worm in your gut, causing your stomach to swell up and cysts to appear in your eyes. The opera singer Maria Callas once had a tapeworm removed from her system. Rumour has it that she purposefully ate the larvae in order to lose weight. But most of her biographers believe she unintentionally got infected by eating raw steak and liver tartare.

Reality Check

Question 1. Researchers have genetically engineered fruit trees that can grow meat. True or false?

Question 2. There's a thriving market for cow urine in India, where many consider it a health drink. True or false?

Question 3. Mineralarians subsist only on foods of mineral origin, believing it to be immoral to eat animal or plant life. True or false?

Question 4. Outhouse Springs Water, a brand of bottled water once sold in the United States, described itself as 'America's first recycled water'. True or false?

Question 5. In 1991 the Kentucky Fried Chicken restaurant chain changed its name to KFC. The reason it did so was to avoid charges of false advertising, because technically the meat it was serving was not chicken. It was actually meat from genetically manipulated organisms lacking beaks, feathers, and feet, and kept alive by tubes inserted into their bodies to pump blood and nutrients throughout their structure. True or false?

Question 6. In 2000 a woman found a breaded, deep-fried chicken's head in a box of McDonald's Chicken Wings. True or false?

Question 7. Cheese made from the milk of lactating rats is considered a delicacy in France. True or false?

Question 8. In 2005 a woman found a human finger in a bowl of chilli served to her at a Wendy's restaurant in California. True or false?

ANSWERS

1. A May 2003 article that circulated online described trees, developed by the bioengineering firm UltraModAgri Group, that supposedly grew meat inside grapefruit. The article quoted a researcher as saying, 'We take the genes from cattle that produce key proteins and splice them into the reproductive cells of grapefruit trees. When the seeds mature into trees, instead of producing ordinary citrus fruit, the pulp contains meat. You get the flavor, texture – even the smell.' As science fiction fans know, gene-splicing technology makes anything possible! Except for meat-growing trees. The source of the article was the *Weekly World News*, an American paper that specialized in spoof news articles. But, strangely enough, a

few months earlier NASA-funded researchers had announced some success at growing meat in a lab dish. So even if we never have meat trees, we may one day have meat-makers sitting on our countertops, growing us fresh chunks of chicken.

2. In India cow urine is called *gomutram*. Aficionados claim that drinking it can treat all manner of illnesses, including cancer and diabetes. Owners of Indian cow shelters have found this health fad quite lucrative. They just filter, bottle, and ship the stuff. The biggest problem apparently is the smell, but that can be masked with herbs and spices. Or just drink it down really fast. Demand is so strong that scam artists find it lucrative to pass off buffalo or sheep urine as authentic cow pee.

3. Mineralarianism was the fanciful creation of Charles Bennett, a researcher at IBM who enjoys creating parody websites in his spare time. He insists he doesn't know any practising Mineralarians. However, there really is a religious group called Breatharians who claim to subsist on light and air. Wiley Brooks has been promoting the practice in the United States since the 1970s, though he admits to occasionally eating hamburgers. (He said pollution was preventing him from getting enough nutrition from air and light.) Several people throughout the world have been found starved to death with copies of Breatharian teachings beside them, examples of Darwinian survival at its finest.

4. True. Billboards for Outhouse Springs Water began appearing around the United States in the summer of 2003, sporting slogans such as 'It's #1, not #2', 'America's first recycled water', and 'Truly Tasteless Water'. At the time, Outhouse Springs Water didn't exist. It was a fictional product dreamed up by the Adams Outdoor ad agency to illustrate the effectiveness of

billboard advertising. But demand for the product became great enough that the agency struck a deal with a bottled-water company to produce a limited run of Outhouse Springs Water for real. This was the rare case in which consumers hoped a product label was false.

5. False. In 1991 Kentucky Fried Chicken did officially change its name to KFC, and soon after an email rumour began to circulate, alleging that the name change occurred because the restaurant was no longer serving 'real' chicken. The email also alluded to a University of New Hampshire study that somehow proved these allegations, and as the rumour gained momentum thousands of worried customers called the university to find out more. However, no such study had been conducted there, and KFC, of course, was not breeding mutant chickens. Officials at the company explained that they had chosen the new name because it was shorter and snappier. Plus, it reduced emphasis on the word 'fried' (with all its unhealthy connotations) and on the word 'chicken' (since the restaurant had introduced an expanded menu that offered far more than chicken).

6. This is apparently true. In November 2000, Katherine Ortega bought a box of chicken wings at her local McDonald's in Newport News, Virginia. (They were 'Mighty Wings' that were being test-marketed in the area rather than Chicken McNuggets, as was often later reported.) But upon taking the meal home, she discovered an unpleasant surprise: a fried chicken head included with the wings. She immediately contacted the media . . . and a lawyer. Reporters who examined the head said the batter on it looked exactly like the batter on the wings, so it didn't seem to be something she had created herself. However, lawyers advised her that suing McDonald's

was unlikely to gain her any money for several reasons. First, she found the head before biting down into it (thus lessening any possibility of claiming psychological trauma), and second, a chicken head is not considered a foreign object if it is found in a box of chicken parts. Therefore a lawsuit never materialized. But the picture of the battered chicken head did become one of the most frequently forwarded email images for the next few years.

7. **False.** The French do love cheese, and they produce a bewildering array of it. But they do not make rodent cheese. Theoretically cheese can be made from the milk of any animal (including humans), but it takes about ten pounds of milk to produce one pound of cheese. Therefore, to produce rat-milk cheese, one would need an awful lot of rats. The website of the 'Federation of Rodent Cheesemakers' alleges that it represents the French rat-cheese industry. It even claims that 'fine rat cheeses are becoming ever more popular'. However, the website is a hoax.

8. **False.** In 2005 Anna Ayala claimed to find a human finger in a bowl of Wendy's chilli. Her allegation received a large amount of media attention and cost Wendy's over $1 million a day in lost sales. However, a police investigation determined that the finger had not been cooked in the chilli, and that it had originally been attached to the hand of a man who worked with Ayala's husband at an asphalt company. Ayala and her husband subsequently pleaded guilty to conspiring to file a false claim. Pretending to find inappropriate objects in food served at restaurants is a popular scam, the goal of which is to extort money from the business. Human body parts, rodents, and condoms are among the objects scammers often pretend to find.

FIVE

Photography

Louis Daguerre announced his invention of the first practical photographic process in 1839. When his discovery was reported in the Philadelphia papers, Dr Bird, a professor of chemistry in that city, was asked what he thought of this new method of copying objects with sunbeams. Dr Bird replied that he thought it all an elaborate hoax. Such a process, in his view, was an 'intrinsic improbability'. Dr Bird, of course, was wrong. Photography was quite real. However, it *was* destined to become one of the greatest tools for hoaxing ever invented.

REALITY RULE 5.1

'Photographs may not lie, but liars may photograph.'*

Adobe's Photoshop brand of image manipulation software has become so widely adopted that 'to photoshop' has entered popular usage as a generic term for doctoring an image, in the same way that Kleenex is a generic term for

---

* Documentary photographer Lewis Hine, 1874–1940.

facial tissue. Adobe objects to this use of the term, insisting that instead of saying, 'The image was photoshopped,' people should say, 'The image was enhanced using Adobe® Photoshop® software.' But to no avail. People keep using the word. In fact, the word has become so popular that many people use it to refer to any fake image whatsoever. This is not only inaccurate but obscures the reality that manipulating an image (whether in the darkroom or on a computer) is not the only way to fake a photo.

The oldest form of photo fakery is one performed before the shutter has even snapped shut. The photographer stages the scene. The first recorded instance of this technique (and simultaneously the first fake photo ever created) dates from 1840. The Frenchman Hippolyte Bayard claimed he

Hippolyte Bayard, Portrait of the Photographer as a Drowned Man.

had invented a photographic process at the same time as Daguerre, yet unlike Daguerre he received no official recognition for his accomplishment. To protest, he took a photo of himself pretending to be a suicide victim, to which he attached a note: 'The Government which has been only too generous to Monsieur Daguerre, has said it can do nothing for Monsieur Bayard, and the poor wretch has drowned himself.'

Even more gruesomely, in 1863 Alexander Gardner took a series of famous photos showing the aftermath of the Battle of Gettysburg. Historians later determined that in some of the photos Gardner had posed a soldier's corpse with a rifle, apparently in an effort to create a more dramatic scene.

Staging continues to be used today, despite the fact that it's considered a cardinal sin of photojournalism. On 20 September 2002, the *New York Times* ran a photo of a young boy of Arabic descent aiming a toy gun outside an Arabian food store in Lackawanna, New York, near to where an alleged al-Qaeda sleeper cell had operated. Pulitzer-winning photographer Ed Keating took the photo, but rival photographers present at the scene accused Keating of staging the shot, claiming he had arranged the scene 'like a fashion shoot'. Keating denied the allegations, and resigned from *The Times*.

A more advanced form of staging involves the use of models. This was the method used for what are arguably the two most famous fake images of all time: the Cottingley Fairies and the Loch Ness Monster 'Surgeon's Photo'. In 1917 two young girls produced what seemed to be photographic evidence of the existence of fairies. Experts carefully examined the photos, but could find no evidence they had been doctored – because they hadn't been. The girls created the images by first sketching fairies, cutting out the figures, and then holding the pieces of paper in place in front of the camera with hatpins. Likewise, the Loch Ness Monster photo, that famous image of a sea serpent's head and neck rising out of the waters of the Loch, was not a product of darkroom tricks. It was a photo of a fake serpent's neck glued onto a toy submarine.

Another way to fake a photo, without altering the image itself, is to attach a phoney caption to it. This can transform a completely innocent image into evidence of the worst barbarity. For instance, in December 1913 the New York *American* ran a photo of a group of children standing in the ocean, their hands raised above their heads. It claimed these children had been herded into the ocean by Mexican soldiers and were about to be shot in the back. But the man who took the picture, Russell Hastings Milward, later protested he had taken the photo while on vacation in British Honduras. The children were happily playing in the surf. They had raised their arms at his request in order to make a better picture.

'*Ocean execution*' (1913).

Advertisers also frequently play fast and loose with captions. In one case, the 'after' picture in a before-and-after weight-loss commercial actually showed the before woman's slender twin sister. Likewise, a 2003 tourism brochure for Bermuda apparently featured images of beaches in Hawaii, scuba divers in the Seychelles, and a woman swimming with a dolphin in Florida. A covered bridge prominently displayed in a Kentucky tourism brochure was actually located in New Hampshire.

Staging the scene and faking the caption are effective methods of faking a photo, but image manipulation remains the most frequently used technique. Photo editors can alter a photo as easily as an artist can put a few more brush strokes on a painting. They can add or delete objects, change a colour, or even move things around. They've always been able to do such things in the darkroom, but software like Photoshop has made it much, much easier. As a result, the phenomenon of photo fakery has grown exponentially during the past three decades.

A notable recent example occurred at the University of Wisconsin-Madison in 2001. Officials there were putting together the undergraduate application brochure. They wanted a photo for the cover that would highlight the diversity of the university, but try as they might they couldn't find any good images of a racially diverse group of UW-Madison students. So they created one. They pasted the smiling face of a black student into a crowd scene taken at a university football game. Then they sent this off to 50,000 potential students. Unfortunately for the school officials, a staffer at the student newspaper noticed that everyone in the picture was in shadow except for the lone black student – who somehow had the sun shining directly on him. Curious, she did some research and soon found the original version of the photo. She then exposed the fake photo on the front page of the school paper. Embarrassed, the university frantically tried to recall all the brochures, but the damage had already been done.

Then there was the infamous Helicopter Shark – one of the most widely circulated images on the Internet in 2002. It showed a great white shark apparently leaping out of the water to attack a military helicopter. An accompanying caption noted that the photo had been 'nominated by *National Geographic* as THE photo of the year'. That wasn't true. However, in 2005 *National Geographic* did publish an article debunking the photo as a fake. An unknown hoaxer

The Helicopter Shark.

had simply pasted a breaching great white shark, taken from an image by photographer Charles Maxwell, into a California National Guard photograph of a US Air Force helicopter hovering in front of the Golden Gate Bridge in San Francisco.

If you're trying to determine whether a photo has been manipulated, there are a number of clues to look for. The first is lighting. Do all the objects in the image appear to be illuminated by the same source of light, or do shadows fall in different directions? Examine the granularity and pixelation of objects. If something appears blockier or grainier than everything around it, it could be because it's been pasted into the photo. Look for repeating patterns caused by use of the cloning tool (a software tool graphic artists use to duplicate parts of a photo). Finally, look for misshapen or missing body parts. Hurried photo forgers inadvertently slice off body parts such as hands or feet with surprising regularity.

However, remember that accurately identifying a fake photo is an art, not a science. It is *very* easy to misinterpret the signs of fakery. For instance, a shadow may be falling in a strange direction because of fakery, or because the surface upon which the shadow is falling is curved. Even experts have difficulty telling the difference, and amateur photo sleuths are invariably far too quick to cry fake. In fact, in this Age of Photoshop, there may no longer be much risk of people being misled by a fake photo. The greater danger is that people now refuse to believe any image is real, even totally legitimate ones.

Should a suitably dramatic picture of a major event not exist, one will be created.

The invention of photography revolutionized the news. Instead of having to imagine events in distant parts of the world, people could see them. Wars and major events came to be defined by the pictures taken of them. An unanticipated side effect of this was that people came to expect every major event to be illustrated by a suitably dramatic photograph. It was as if, without the visual aid of the photograph, people no longer knew how to react to an event. But what if no photographer was present? No matter. Thanks to the efforts of photo fakers, a photograph would inevitably appear anyway.

This phenomenon can be traced back to as early as 1857 when a rebellion in India was savagely put down by British forces. No one captured the battle itself on film, but the photographer Felice Beato arrived on the scene a couple of months later, after the dead had already been buried. Unfazed, he arranged for bodies to be disinterred so he could recreate the battle scene strewn with bones.

Later, the Soviets proved to be masters of conjuring photos of historically significant events out of thin air. The Bloody Sunday massacre of 1905, when Russian police opened fire on protesting workers in St Petersburg, was one of the key events that led to the downfall of the Tsarist regime. For decades, a sensational photo of this event appeared in Soviet textbooks, showing a line of soldiers opening fire as workers fled. What the textbooks never acknowledged was that the photo showed a re-enactment staged for a propaganda film twenty years after

The faux Bloody Sunday Massacre.

the fact. In reality, there were no good photographs taken of the massacre itself.

In recent times, the Internet has become the premier source for photographs of unphotographed events. Almost immediately after 11 September 2001, a photo began circulating online showing a man posing on the observation deck of the World Trade Center, while, unbeknownst to him, a hijacked plane approached from behind. A caption accompanying the image read: 'Attached is a picture that was taken of a tourist atop the World Trade Center Tower, the first to be struck by a terrorist attack. This camera was found but the subject in the picture has not yet been located.' If real, it was a remarkable photo, capturing the tragedy from a victim's perspective. But it wasn't real. It turned out to be the work of a Hungarian man who had created it as a joke for his friends, never intending it to circulate as widely as it did.

The World Trade Center Man, aka Tourist Guy.

Two years later, no cameras recorded the explosion of the space shuttle Columbia, but that didn't stop the spread of a dramatic series of images supposedly taken by 'an Israeli satellite in space'. The pictures were actually still images from the Touchstone Pictures movie *Armageddon*. In the movie there is a scene in which meteorite fragments strike a space shuttle. An unknown hoaxer had simply lifted images from this scene, added a phoney caption, and set the pictures loose online.

On 14 August 2003, a blackout hit the north-eastern United States. Almost the next day a photo appeared claiming to be a NASA satellite image of the event. The entire United States could be seen, with dots of light revealing major population centres . . . except for the north-eastern corner of the country, which was covered in inky blackness. The picture (minus the blacked-out portion) was a real satellite image

Satellite photo of blackout.

Tsunami seen from a high-rise.

that had appeared on NASA's Astronomy Picture of the Day website, but not in 2003. It dated back to November 2000. (And it was actually a composite image of hundreds of photos taken by Defense Department meteorological satellites.) A hoaxer had darkened the relevant portion of the photo to make it appear to show the blackout.

Finally, after the Asian tsunami of December 2004, a picture circulated showing an enormous wave, hundreds of feet high, bearing down on a city. The caption read: 'This picture is not a fake. It appears to have been taken from a hi-rise building window in downtown Phuket Thailand. The power of nature is hard to comprehend, especially the destructiveness of water.' Except that the city in the photo wasn't Phuket. It was Antofagasta, Chile. The gigantic wave had been photoshopped in.

Whatever disaster may lie in the future, you can guarantee you'll find dramatic photos of it online. You just can't guarantee the photos will be real.

Reality Check

Question 1.
A vapour cone forms around a jet plane as it breaks the sound barrier. Real or fake?

Question 2. A camel spider found in Iraq. Real or fake?

Question 3.
Snowball the
'Monster Cat',
held in the arms
of its owner.
Real or fake?

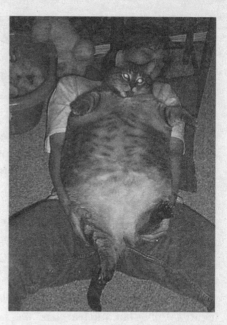

Question 4.
Munchkin the cat.
Real or fake?

ANSWERS

1. It almost looks too cool to be real, but the photo is authentic. This shot of an F/A-18 Hornet assigned to Strike Fighter Squadron One Five One (VFA-151) was taken over the Pacific on 7 July 1999 by Ensign John Gay. As it circulated on the Internet, the image was often described as 'a picture of a sonic boom', which is somewhat misleading. The vapour cone forming around the plane is not a sonic boom. It's caused by the extreme speed of the plane pressurizing the air and causing the moisture in it to condense. In other words, a plane doesn't have to break the sound barrier in order to cause a vapour cone to form, though in this photo the plane reportedly was about to do so.

2. Camel spiders are real. They do live in Iraq. They are big and nasty looking. And this image, which began circulating online in 2004, wasn't digitally manipulated. However, a caption that accompanied the image was misleading. It stated that camel spiders 'latch on and inject you with a local anaesthesia so you can't feel it feeding on you. They eat flesh, not just suck out your juices like a normal spider.' This was not true. Camel spiders are non-venomous and do not feed on humans. Their preferred food is crickets, woodlice, and scorpions.

3. The Internet loves fat cats (or tub cats, as they're sometimes called), and the first big cat to become an Internet celebrity was Snowball, the 'Monster Cat', whose picture first appeared in inboxes in early 2000. An accompanying story told how Snowball's mother had been found abandoned near a Canadian nuclear lab, the implication being that Snowball's size (87 pounds supposedly) was the result of genetic mutation. In reality, Snowball was the digital creation of Washington-state resident Cordell Hauglie (the man in the picture). Hauglie had 'improved' a picture of the family cat Jumper as a joke to share with his daughter, but his daughter forwarded it to her friends, and they forwarded it to their friends, and so on and so on. Somewhere along the line a prankster added the bogus story about the nuclear lab. Having never intended his tall-tale photo to spread as far as it did, Hauglie reports that he almost fell out of his chair when he saw the picture featured on his local evening news. He had no idea it (and he) had become so famous.

4. This picture of 'Munchkin' began circulating online in 2002. No story accompanied the image, but that didn't stop it from achieving Internet fame. The *Sydney Morning Herald* declared the picture to be a hoax, but Munchkin turned out to be that rare curiosity – a real fat cat. In 2005 his owner, Susan Martin of Ontario, Canada, posted more pictures of her 'fatboy' to prove he was real. His actual name was Sassy; he weighed 40 pounds; and he had died of heart disease. At 40 pounds Sassy was certainly a very big boy, but he didn't qualify as the fattest cat ever. That honour goes to Katy, a Siamese living in the Ural Mountains, who tipped the scales at over 50 pounds. However, Katy's achievement remained unofficial because the *Guinness Book of World Records* does not maintain a category for fattest cat. It doesn't want to encourage people to overfeed their pets.

SIX

The World Wide Web

In the language of the Internet, to be 'pwned' means to be owned, or hoaxed. According to legend, the term was first used during an online game when a winning player tried to type 'You Were Owned' but misspelled it as 'You Were Pwned'. The term has been in use ever since. (How to pronounce it is anyone's guess.) As you navigate the World Wide Web, the constant challenge is to go about your business without getting pwned.

REALITY RULE 6.1

Just because you read it on the Internet, doesn't mean it's true.

The Internet places a vast amount of information at your fingertips. In fact, it gives you access to more information than was ever available to any researcher throughout human history. The Great Library of Alexandria pales in comparison. But with so much information it becomes more important than ever to realize that not all of it is of equal value. The reliability of the source must be considered. After all, information is only as good as its source.

The tendency to believe any information found on the Internet, no matter how far-fetched, is sometimes called 'Pierre Salinger syndrome'. The name derives from an incident that occurred in July 1996, when TWA Flight 800 crashed into the Atlantic Ocean just south of Long Beach. Four months later, the journalist Pierre Salinger stated at a press conference that the plane had been downed by friendly fire from US Forces. Official investigators immediately denied this claim, but Salinger insisted he had proof. And what was his proof? An apparently random document he had come across on the Internet. Salinger denied all this, insisting he got the information from an offline source, but the phrase stuck. The first use of it is attributed to *Wired* reporter Moira Gunn in a July 1997 article.

A good rule of thumb is that you can trust information from accredited news sources such as CNN or the BBC. (There are some major qualifications to that statement which will be discussed in Chapter Ten.) However sometimes information looks like it comes from an accredited news source, when it doesn't really.

In late 2002, sixteen-year-old Eric Smith and a friend created the Fake CNN News Generator. Visitors to this website could type text and a headline into a form, which instantly formatted the material to look like a CNN news page, complete with authentic CNN logo and banner ads. It was a recipe for chaos waiting to be unleashed.

Smith and his friend later claimed they never intended for the public to discover their creation. But in early 2003 word of the fake news generator leaked out, and almost overnight it was receiving over two million visitors a day. That's when the chaos began.

Thousands of phoney news stories began to circulate on the Internet, where they did their evil work. One story fooled a number of TV and radio stations into reporting that the (still living) musician Dave Matthews had died of a drug overdose. Another story claimed the American child stars the Olsen Twins had decided to attend the University of Notre Dame, causing the office of admissions to be flooded by phone calls from particularly obsessive fans of the teen celebrities. (The Olsens eventually went to New York University.) At first the media had no idea where these fake stories were coming from, but then they traced them to the fake CNN news generator. CNN quickly had the site shut down.

The CNN fake news generator remains the most notorious phoney news creator of all time, but there are still plenty of others out there, capable of mimicking any reputable news site including the Associated Press, the *New York Times*, or the BBC. This is why you can't assume a news story on the Internet is true – even if it looks official. Clues that a story might be the work of a prankster include bad grammar, poor spelling, and strange-looking URLs – for instance, if the story isn't posted at cnn.com, but at some variant of that address such as world-cnn.com. The best defence against fake news is to check that other sources are reporting the same story before you run and tell all your friends about the incredible thing you just read on the Internet.

Although the Internet may be home to an enormous amount of misinformation, the good news is that it is simultaneously home to an enormous amount of accurate information. In fact, it's the greatest tool for debunking misinformation ever created. Which is why – to use the language of the Internet once again – before you make an uninformed, inaccurate claim, you should always first go online and 'fact check your ass'.

Anyone can create a website.

As you surf the web, you'll find all kinds of unusual sites. One day you may stumble upon the homepage of the Society for the Protection and Preservation of Fruitcakes (fruitcakesociety.org). The next day you'll discover the website of the Institute of Advanced Rutabaga Studies members.tripod.com/~rutabagas). The Fruitcake Society is real (it's an informal group of people who like fruitcakes) while the Rutabaga Institute is not. But how would you know this? Given the number of hoax sites to be found on the web, how can you know whether any website is real or fake (fake meaning in this context that it claims to be something other than what it really is)? It's not easy.

The first thing to remember is that you should never try to judge a website on its appearance alone. Just because a site looks professionally designed does not mean it's the genuine homepage of a real organization. As the reality rule states, *anyone* can create a website.

In order to differentiate the real from the fake, it helps to be familiar with the ten varieties of hoax websites. Nine are listed below. The tenth (fake weblogs) is described later in this chapter. (Note: I make no guarantee that any of the URLs provided will still work by the time you read this.)

#1. The Practical Joke. Would you believe there's such a thing as dehydrated water (buydehydratedwater.com), or a campaign to save the Pacific Northwest Tree Octopus (zapatopi.net/treeoctopus)? Hopefully not. But sites advancing these and other tongue-in-cheek claims can be found across the web. They're harmless jokes, attempting nothing more sinister than to pull your leg, and common sense should help you spot them. But if not, look for the telltale T-shirt sale. Practical joke sites are often created as a way to lure people in with a bit of humour and then sell them merchandise such as T-shirts, caps, mugs, etc.

As far-fetched as such sites can be, someone is always gullible enough to believe them. For instance, in 2004 the city council of Aliso Viejo, California, deliberated on whether to ban products made with the chemical dihydrogen monoxide, after finding a website (dhmo.org) that detailed the dangers of this 'odourless, tasteless chemical'. The site warned that this chemical is a major component of acid rain, that it corrodes metal, and that its ingestion causes excessive sweating and urination – all of which sounded really bad to the council. Thankfully, before it could embarrass itself further, someone clued them in that dihydrogen monoxide is the scientific term for water.

Some other practical joke sites to check out: Dog Island, the island where dogs roam free (thedogisland.com); Rent a German, 'Rent a German . . . and smile!' (rentagerman.de); and Flatulent Technologies, 'extracting energy from everything that stinks or rots' (flatulenttechnologies.com).

#2. The Parody. Parody is mockery by comic imitation. Usually parodies are obvious enough, because of the exaggerated or distorted nature of the imitation. But sometimes they're far more subtle, in which case they acquire the attributes of a hoax. Hands down, the most successful hoax/parody on the web to date was Objective: Christian Ministries (its URL now leads to a dating service). On first, second, and third glance it appeared to be a site run by a group of earnest fundamentalist Christians who advocated policies such as redesigning the American flag to include the word GOD stamped across it. They also condemned Apple Computer as a 'front for evolutionism'. The site fooled almost everyone, including fundamentalists. For a while it conned a Christian web-hosting service into providing it with space on their server. In reality, it was an elaborate anti-Christian spoof, rumoured to have ties to a porn operator.

Some other parody sites to check out: Whitehouse.org, a political parody of Whitehouse.gov (the official site of the White House); and preparingforemergencies.co.uk, Thomas Scott's spoof of the British government's Preparing for Emergencies site (preparingforemergencies.gov.uk). Scott's version prepares citizens for emergencies such as zombie attacks and alien invasions, but the comedy was lost on British authorities who unsuccessfully attempted to force Scott to take his site down.

#3. **The Gross-Out or Shock Hoax.** Bonsaikitten.com describes how to raise kittens inside glass jars so that the kittens' bones mould to the shapes of the jars. The site even claims to sell these 'bonsai kittens'. But thankfully the site is a hoax, created as a prank in late 2000 by some MIT students. No kittens were harmed in its creation. The FBI officially determined this after receiving thousands of complaints.

Bonsaikitten.com is the most notorious example of a gross-out hoax website. The goal of such sites is simple – to shock and disturb. They flourish on the web for three reasons. First, they're simple to create; second, they have built-in

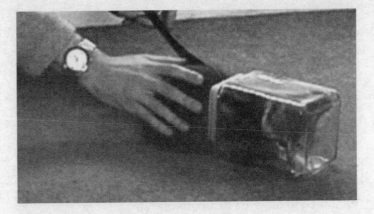

Bonsai kitten.

credibility since people do disgusting and cruel things, for real, every day; and third, they provide an easy way for someone who wants to attract attention (even negative attention) to get it.

Another infamous gross-out site (now offline) was cutoffmyfeet.com, on which a man named Freck claimed he was going to host a live broadcast of himself cutting off his feet. There was also manbeef.com, which claimed to sell cuts of human flesh 'for the sophisticated human meat consumer'.

A clue that a shocking site is a hoax is if it claims to sell something such as bonsai kittens or human flesh, but doesn't actually provide a means to purchase the product. Also, if the site offers to sell you a T-shirt or mug, that is, as always, a sign of a hoax.

Some other gross-out sites to check out: Celebrity Skin, the online source for celebrity skin and bodily fluids (blackpitchpress.com/celebrityskin); and PetsOrFood.com, which claims to sell a range of species including bald eagles,

Man beef.

snakes, hamsters, and baby seals, all delivered live or 'ready to eat'.

#4. Movie Promotions. In 1999 the *Blair Witch Project* became a multi-million-dollar box-office sensation thanks to a clever marketing scheme centred around a hoax website (blairwitch.com) that claimed the Blair Witch was real. Visitors to the site could read detailed pseudo-historical background information about her, all of which seemed authentic enough to convince thousands of people of her reality. Ever since then movie promoters have been enamoured of hoax websites. One of the more successful post-*Blair Witch* efforts was the Blonde Legal Defense Club website (nationalblondeday.com), which described the group as dedicated to stopping 'the widespread belief that blondes are dumb and incapable'. To achieve this goal the BLDC declared 9 July 'National Blonde Day'. In reality the site was a publicity stunt for the Reese Witherspoon movie *Legally Blonde*.

Some other movie-related sites to check out: Godsend Institute.org, a Massachusetts fertility clinic offering human cloning services (from 2004's *Godsend*); and LacunaInc.com, a company devoted to non-surgical memory erasure (from 2004's *Eternal Sunshine of the Spotless Mind*).

#5. Covert Ad Campaigns. Mainstream marketers were slightly slower than their counterparts in the movie industry to realize how hoax websites could create buzz around a product. But they've recently played catch-up, and now disguised advertising campaigns are all over the Internet. One of the most elaborate to date was the homepage of engineering genius Colin Mayhew, who detailed his efforts to build a humanoid crash-preventing 'autonomous robot' out of the body of a BMW Mini Cooper. A dubious-sounding project, until you viewed the remarkable video of his robot stopping a car in its tracks moments before it would have slammed into a wall. Those looking for more details about Mayhew soon uncovered a complex web of Internet references to humanoid robots, including a book titled *Men of Metal: Eyewitness Accounts of Humanoid Robots* on the website of Casson Publishing (now offline). But in reality the Mini Cooper Autonomous Robot, Colin Mayhew, and Casson Publishing were all part of a viral marketing campaign dreamed up by the ad agency Crispin Porter & Bogusky. What were they advertising? The new BMW Mini Cooper, obviously.

Since 2008, the popularity of video-sharing sites such as YouTube have led advertisers to focus more on hoax videos than hoax websites. One of the biggest successes in this genre was 2008's mobile phone popcorn video, which purported to show popcorn being cooked by mobile phones. A few kernels of popcorn were placed in between three mobile phones on

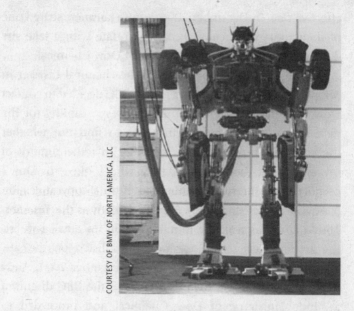

The Mini Cooper Autonomous Robot.

a table. The mobile phones dialled each other, and the kernels instantly began to pop. This turned out to be part of a marketing campaign for a maker of Bluetooth headsets, Cardo Systems.

Some other covert ad campaigns to check out: Derrie-Air Airlines (flyderrie-air.com), the airline that charges passengers based on their weight (it's really a front for a media conglomerate that wanted to demonstrate its effectiveness at promoting brands); and Elite Designers Against IKEA (elitedesigners.org), an anti-IKEA site created by IKEA itself.

#6. Culture Jammers. Culture Jammers are activists who use hoaxes both to expose corporate hypocrisy and to get people thinking about issues of social justice. Creating hoax websites is just one of their methods, but it's proven an amazingly effective one. In December 2004 culture jammers scored one of their most spectacular successes to date with a fake site designed to look like the homepage of Dow Chemical.

As the twentieth anniversary of the chemical disaster in Bhopal approached, journalists at the BBC decided to contact Dow Chemical (which had inherited responsibility for the disaster via a corporate acquisition) to find out whether the company planned to do anything in remembrance of the event. But the BBC journalists who looked for Dow's corporate website instead stumbled upon a copycat version (dowethics.com) created by a group known as the Yes Men. Thinking it was real, the journalists sent an email requesting an interview to the media contact listed on the site. The Yes Men happily obliged. On 3 December 2004, Andy Bichlbaum of the Yes Men appeared on the BBC disguised as 'Jude Finisterra' of Dow Chemical and proceeded to announce that Dow had decided to pay $12 billion in compensation to the Bhopal victims. Dow's stock value promptly dropped. Only later that day, after Dow called the BBC to complain that the company had no idea who Mr Finisterra was, did the BBC realize it had been culture jammed.

Another culture jamming site to check out: Gatt.org, homepage of the World Trade Organization as imagined by the Yes Men. In 2000 it fooled the Center for International Legal Studies into inviting a speaker from the site to a conference on international services. The Yes Men sent 'Dr Bichlbauer', who lectured the other attendees about the poor work habits of Italians and proposed that Americans should sell their votes to the highest bidder.

#7. Art Projects. Artists sometimes create elaborate fake websites for the sheer challenge of making the imaginary appear real, and also to make audiences think about the boundaries between fact and fiction. Take Clubbo.com, the purported home on the web of indie record label Clubbo. On the site you'll find biographies of the bands Clubbo has supposedly represented as well as generous samples of their music. It's the songs that make Clubbo seem real. They're catchy, their production value is high, and they seem strikingly representative of the eras in which they were recorded. That someone would have invented them all as a hoax seems inconceivable. But someone did. San Francisco artists Elise Malmberg and Joe Gore created Clubbo as a light-hearted experiment in web fiction. Once you realize the whole thing is fake it's fun to go back and appreciate the songs as a kind of masterful yet subtle send-up of the history of pop music.

Some other art projects to check out: the Emily Chesley Reading Circle (emilychesley.com), dedicated to promoting the work of a 'speculative' Canadian author; and Boilerplate (bigredhair.com/boilerplate), the history of a Victorian-era robot.

#8. Alternative Reality Games. Ilovebees.com appeared to be the website of a small, family-owned bee farm called Margaret's Honey. But after visitors spent a few seconds on the site, strange things began to occur. Warning messages flashed: MODULE CORE HEMORRHAGE, SYSTEM PERIL DISTRIBUTED REFLEX. What visitors had stumbled upon wasn't actually the homepage of a honey company. It was the starting point (or 'rabbit hole') for an Alternative Reality Game (or ARG). ARGs are role-playing games acted out in real-life settings. Players follow clues that may involve digging up a buried treasure, meeting a stranger on a street corner, responding to an email, or visiting a strange website. In the case of I Love Bees, some players received clue-containing jars of honey in the mail. Others had to answer payphones in specific places at specific times. These hints led them to a mystery involving rogue military artificial-intelligence pro-grammes, time-travelling soldiers, and interstellar warfare.

What this means for those of us who aren't ARGers, is that we may come across websites of companies or organi-zations that look real, but are actually part of an ARG. Nowadays many ARGs are created by advertisers, hoping to hook consumers with a fun game. I Love Bees, for instance, was part of the marketing effort for the Xbox game *Halo 2*.

Another ARG to check out: dionaea-house.com. It appears to be a weblog but develops into a spooky ARG about a flesh-eating house. It was designed to promote a movie screenplay written by Eric Heisserer.

#9. The Scam. The web is no stranger to scams. Typically, con artists use fake websites to put a veneer of credibility on businesses that are disreputable or don't exist. In 2003 inves-tigators discovered a copycat version of the Better Business Bureau's site identical to the real thing in every way except for one detail – whereas the real BBB site had no reference to a securities-broker firm named Parker Jennings, the fake site not only listed it but also gave it an excellent customer-satisfaction rating. Apparently Parker Jennings had been directing potential clients who asked for a reference to its own personal BBB. The case prompted the BBB to remind consumers that on the Internet 'things are not always as they seem'. Indeed.

Instead of directing you to an actual scam, check out McWhortle Enterprises (mcwhortle.com), homepage of a (non-existent) company promoting a new 'bio-hazard detector'. The American Securities and Exchange Commission created the site in 2002 as a way to demonstrate to investors the danger of online investing fraud.

On the Internet, nobody knows you're a dog.

A cartoon published in the *New Yorker* magazine in 1993 shows a dog sitting in front of a computer. To a second canine seated on the floor he remarks, 'On the Internet, nobody knows you're a dog.'

It's a good observation. The anonymity of cyberspace allows people (or dogs) to present themselves in any way they want . . . as anybody they want. There's very little way of knowing if people really are who they say they are. As a more cynical saying puts it, 'On the Internet the men are men, the women are men, and the children are FBI agents.'

It's particularly common to encounter false identities on personal weblogs (online diaries). Bloggers often present themselves to the world as someone else – someone more interesting, someone whose life other people might actually want to read about. Lesbians, prostitutes, celebrities, hot girls, and people dying of terminal illnesses are among the most popular alter egos. By contrast, out-of-work (non-lesbian) accountants, (non-lesbian) grocery baggers, and awkward teenage boys are not popular alter egos.

Fake public journals, which is what faux weblogs are, are not entirely new. In 1722 a series of letters supposedly written by a middle-aged widow named Silence Dogood appeared in the Boston-based *New-England Courant*. Silence described her life and the difficulties she endured as a single mother. Readers loved her. In fact, a few of them wrote in asking for her hand in marriage. Silence declined these offers since she was, in reality, a sixteen-year-old boy named Benjamin Franklin (yes, *the* Benjamin Franklin).

Then there was the survival diary of Joe Knowles. In 1913 Knowles walked alone and naked into the Maine woods. His challenge was to survive unaided for two months. So the public could follow his progress, he scratched out daily diary entries on pieces of bark that were picked up by a *Boston Post* reporter at a pre-arranged drop-off site and then published in the paper. He emerged from the woods a national hero. Only years later was it learned that he had spent the two months in a log cabin, sunning himself, and feasting on cherry pie.

The Internet revolutionized the fake public diary genre by making it so easy to do, and so easy to get attention by doing it. Suddenly hundreds (perhaps thousands) of people, who would never have considered keeping a diary, were online writing fake ones.

The first fake web diary to gain lots of attention (at a time before the word 'blog' was widely used) was that of Kaycee Nicole Swenson. Kaycee presented herself as a nineteen-year-old girl dying of leukaemia. People were so genuinely moved by her valiant struggle against her illness that when she died of a brain aneurysm on 15 May 2001, they wanted to attend her funeral. That's when things started to get strange, because Kaycee's mother refused to allow anyone at the funeral. The reason why soon became apparent. Kaycee had never existed. She was the fictional creation of her 'mother', forty-year-old Debbie Swenson.

The exposure of Kaycee Nicole was big news. At the time, there hadn't been a case quite like it. Since then fake online diaries have become fairly common. One of the more sensational faux-blog-outings was the unmasking of Plain Layne, an attractive young woman whose weblog read like a fast-paced soap opera. Layne's adventures included taking off for Mexico (where she became a lesbian), finding one of her birth parents, and seducing a straight co-worker (after she became a lesbian). It was titilating stuff, read by thousands of people, except that Layne was really Odin Soli, a thirty-something male entrepreneur with a heart condition.

Companies have noticed the blogging phenomenon and jumped into the fray with faux-blogs of their own. 'Ted's Life at Amazon' was supposedly the online journal of Amazon.com employee Ted (he never revealed his last name), who posted offbeat entries about what it was like to work for the web retailer. One of his insights was, 'This is a cheap place.' But one day his blog was replaced by an Amazon recruiting page. When readers tried to find out what had happened, an Amazon representative admitted Ted's journal had been 'a recruiting message that we put in the form of a blog to experiment'. The remark that Amazon was a cheap place must have been an attempt to sound true-to-life.

If you can't trust the identity of bloggers, nor can you trust the identity of the millions of people to be found in chat rooms and message boards. One unhappily married Jordanian man, Bakr Melhem, found out the hard way about the treachery of online identity. As reported by Jordan's *Petra* news agency, Melhem began posing as a bachelor named Adnan in a chat room for singles. Soon he had struck up a cyber relationship with a woman named Jamila, who was everything he wanted in a woman. But when he suggested they meet in person, tragedy struck. Melhem went to the bus depot where he had arranged to meet his cyber flame, only to find waiting none other than his wife (aka 'Jamila'). His wife was just as shocked to see 'Adnan' as he was to see her. (There is a possibility this is an urban legend reported as news; see Chapter Ten.)

There are even restless souls who aren't content to adopt one alter ego online. They want to be many different people . . . *at the same time.* The most notorious case occurred in 2001 when the San Francisco craigslist message board was set abuzz by a picture of a handsome man standing at a local bus stop. Who was this 'gorgeous guy', everybody wanted to know. The more people posted about Gorgeous Guy, the more attention the discussion attracted – until thousands of people were engrossed by the mystery, earning the phenomenon a spot in many newspapers as well as on CNN.

But when journalist David Cassel did a little spadework, he discovered that many of the people posting about Gorgeous Guy shared an IP address (an identification number assigned to every computer online). Either all these people were using the same computer, or one person was posting messages under different aliases. Who was the owner of this computer? Gorgeous Guy himself. Gorgeous Guy maintained that the messages were posted by his co-workers as a prank. Either way, all was not as it originally appeared to be.

Vanity, as in the case of Gorgeous Guy, may be one motive for faking an online identity. Another is good, old-fashioned financial gain. This is particularly apparent in the many fake reviews that pepper retail sites such as Amazon.com. In February 2004 a technical glitch unmasked the people who had posted anonymous book reviews on the website of the Canadian division of Amazon.com, revealing that many reviews had been written by spouses, relatives, and friends of the author, or by the authors themselves. Which is why Amazon reviews should be taken with a heavy grain of salt.

Creating a phoney identity in order to write a glowing review of your own book, or to serve as an ally during an online debate, is known as creating a 'sock puppet'. An elaborate case of sock puppetry was exposed in 2003 when it was revealed that a prominent conservative scholar, John Lott Jr, had been posting messages and reviews about his own work under the pseudonym 'Mary Rosh'. Rosh passionately praised Lott's book in her review on Amazon.com. In cyber forums discussing Lott, she invariably showed up to defend the scholar's work. She described herself as a former student of his at the University of Pennsylvania, saying he was 'the best professor I ever had' and 'there were a group of us students who would try to take any class that he taught'.

Rosh continued this online campaign on Lott's behalf for almost three years, until a Cato Institute staffer named Julian Sanchez grew suspicious. Sanchez compared Rosh's IP address (recorded when she made posts to online forums) to Lott's IP address (which Sanchez obtained from an email Lott had once sent him). They were one and the same. Sanchez posted this information on his weblog, commenting, 'We're a little old to be playing dress up, aren't we Dr Lott?'

Lott confessed that Mary Rosh was indeed his online alter ego, explaining in his defence, 'I get attacked a lot and I don't want to spend all of my time defending myself.' Presumably Lott didn't consider the hours he spent as Mary Rosh 'his time'. Lott also insisted he had not written the Amazon review, but attributed that literary effort to his wife and one of his sons. (To the accused, it's subtle distinctions like these that make all the difference.)

Most disturbingly of all, the person you're chatting with online may not even be a person. He or she may be a robot. For instance, Mark V. Shaney was the screen name of a frequent contributor to the net.singles usenet group during the 1980s. Shaney's off-the-wall remarks led many to conclude he was a little weird. But it was later revealed that Shaney was actually a Bell Labs computer program that used a Markov Chain algorithm (thus the name of the character) to generate text based on previously appearing word combinations. The program came up with semi-comprehensible statements such as, 'Oh, sorry. Nevermind. I am afraid of it becoming another island in a nice suit.' Given the number of semi-comprehensible statements made by 'real' participants in the group, few people guessed Shaney was just lines of code.

In a similar case, between 2003 and 2004 hundreds of online Romeos were lured into talking with a sexy-sounding nineteen-year-old Californian who called herself VixenLove. VixenLove, like Mark V. Shaney, often seemed a little spaced-out, but that didn't deter the guys who were thrilled to find a girl online. Except that she wasn't a girl. She was a computer program designed to simulate human responses. VixenLove is no longer online, but you never know when one of her sisters might log on. To paraphrase the reality rule, 'On the Internet, nobody knows you're an artificial intelligence program.'

Reality Check

Question 1. The energy company PowerGen registered the domain name powergenitalia.com for its Italian subsidiary, not realizing the URL could be read in two ways. True or false?

Question 2. Denver resident Alek Komarnitsky allows all 17,000 of the Christmas lights on his house to be controlled by web users. True or false?

Question 3. The 'Spud Server' website is hosted on a server powered entirely by potatoes. True or false?

1. Sometimes names that are perfectly innocent when written normally acquire whole new shades of meaning when strung together as URLs. But in this case, powergenitalia.com was not the result of an oversight by the PowerGen company. It was an unknown prankster's joke. When the URL started making the rounds on the Internet in mid-2004, Power-Gen was quick to disassociate itself from it. However, many companies and organizations *have* failed to see the double meanings of their domain names. Some examples: viagrafix.com (home of ViaGrafix), ipwine.com (home of the Ingleside Vineyard), whorepresents.com (home of Who Represents), cummingfirst.com (home of the Cumming First United Methodist Church located in Cumming, Georgia), and rightsexchange.com (home of Rights Exchange, a firm specializing in digital rights management applications). Of course, some organizations intentionally have a bit of fun with their domain names – the classic example being nice-tits.org, official site of the Royal Tit-Watching (Ornithological) Society of Britain.

2. Alek Komarnitsky's web-controlled Christmas lights are an example of a hoax that, by popular demand, became a reality. So whether you answered true or false, you were correct. Alek first brought his Christmas lights online during the 2002 holiday season, and by 2004 they had become something of a web tradition. Millions of people were surfing over to his site to play with them. But the reality was that visitors to his site had no control over the lights. The 'webcam' video was just a series of computer-generated images. Even the details that many people noticed – such as the garage door occasionally being open, or a car passing by, or an airplane flying overhead – were programmed special effects. Alek finally confessed the hoax to a reporter from the *Wall Street Journal*. But in subsequent years, Alek felt so bad about what he had done that he decided to make the web-controlled Christmas lights a reality, and this time people checked to make sure he wasn't lying. Alek uses the publicity the lights attract to raise money for coeliac disease research at the University of Maryland.

3. Potatoes can be a source of electricity. Therefore it is theoretically possible to run a web server on potato-power. All you need is enough potatoes, and someone crazy enough to string them together. Given this world's abundant supply of both potatoes and crazy people, it seemed only a matter of time before someone made the spud server a reality, and in early 2000 news of a functioning spud server circulated around the Internet. The BBC and *USA Today* both reported it. But, alas, the spud was a dud. It was a hoax created by a band of web pranksters called Temple ov Thee Lemur. However, the hoax did inspire a man named Fredric White to build a real spud server, which he brought online in June 2000. He soon pulled the plug on it after growing disgusted by the smell of rotting potatoes. Also, the potatoes didn't power the entire server, only the server's CPU – since, as White noted, powering the entire server would have required over one thousand potatoes. White's effort is the closest anyone has come to creating a potato-powered web server.

SEVEN

Email

In some parallel universe, all email is true. Everyone there is a millionaire because Bill Gates really does pay out hundreds of dollars each time someone forwards a message to a friend, and the penis and breast enhancement formulas that spammers hawk have given everyone superhuman body proportions. But here in this world, it's wiser to trust nothing in your inbox.

REALITY RULE 7.1

No trick, ploy, or scheme is beneath the dignity of a spammer.

Spam, in its original incarnation, was a brand of canned pork marketed by Hormel Foods. The word was an abbreviation of Shoulder Pork and hAM. People began to use the term to refer to junk email and Internet postings during the early 1980s. This usage had nothing to do with the meat itself, but rather derived from a *Monty Python* skit in which Vikings in a restaurant chant the word 'spam' repetitively over and over again. The junk messages that flood our inboxes are similarly repetitive and obnoxious.

Spam comes in a number of varieties. For instance, 'spam-ouflage' is junk email that has been camouflaged, usually by deceptive wording of the subject line, to look like legitimate correspondence. 'Fried spam' is a junk message forwarded to you by a friend (i.e. 'friend spam'). Often this takes the form of bogus warnings that your friend mistakenly thinks it will be helpful to forward to everyone.

In order to battle spam, software designers have created filtering programs that attempt to automatically identify spam and delete it. Unfortunately, these programs don't always identify messages correctly, resulting in 'ham' – legitimate email mistaken for spam.

Spammers fight back against these filtering programs by trying to disguise their messages. One strategy is to string together random words, forming text that is meaningless to a human, but looks like an authentic message to a filtering program. This gibberish text is called 'spamku', which stands for spam haiku.

Another strategy spammers use is to misspell keywords that filtering programs look for – words such as Viagra. The software makers, aware of this strategy, update their software to check for common misspellings, and the spammers respond by making their misspellings ever more creative. Rob Cockerham, webmaster of cockeyed.com, calculated that there are over 600,426,974,379,824,381,952 different ways to misspell Viagra. (V1agra, Vi@gra, vi*agra, v*i*a*g*r*a, etc.). So this is a battle the spammers will likely win.

Spammers practise their obnoxious trade for a simple reason. It's profitable. It costs them almost nothing to send out a million emails, and if only one person out of this million responds to their offer to buy low-cost pharmaceutical products, they've made money.

However, profit is not *always* the motive of spammers. An unusual case that occurred in 2003 raised the possibility that some spammers do what they do because they're completely insane.

Millions of people received the following message:

Hello, I'm a time traveler stuck here in 2003. Upon arriving here my dimensional warp generator stopped working . . . I am going to need a new DWG unit, prefereably the rechargeable AMD wrist watch model with the GRC79 induction motor, four I80200 warp stabilizers, 512GB of SRAM, and the menu driven GUI with front panel XID display. I will take whatever model you have in stock, as long as its received certification for being safe on carbon based life forms. In terms of payment: I dont have any Galactic Credits left. Payment can be made in platinum gold or 2003 currency upon safe delivery of unit.

This message generated enormous curiosity and speculation on the web. Recipients didn't know what to make of it. Was it a bizarre hoax or joke? A deviously sophisticated form of spamouflage designed to trick them into buying something? A marketing ploy to harvest their email address? A publicity stunt for an upcoming book, movie, or video game? Or was it a real plea for help from a stranded time traveller?

A few recipients responded to the message and found, to their surprise, that the stranded time traveller answered back. Politely, never breaking out of character, he repeated his request for a DWG unit. No matter how hard he was pressed, he didn't budge.

A few pranksters went one better and tried to fulfil the time traveller's request. Dimensional generators appeared for sale on eBay, and an online Alien Technology Catalog offered not only dimensional warp generators, but also quantum computing processors, portable fusion generators, and time transduction capacitors. Everything a time traveller could desire. Unfortunately, the time travelling spammer never took the bait.

Finally, in late 2003, *Wired* reporter Brian McWilliams tracked the messages to a house in Woburn, Massachusetts occupied by Robert 'Roddy' Todino. McWilliams got Todino on the phone and asked him, 'Have you been sending out hundreds of millions of emails requesting a dimensional warp generator?' 'Yes,' Todino admitted. 'Why?' McWilliams inquired.

Todino's response was matter of fact. He explained that he needed a dimensional warp generator to get back home . . . and if malevolent forces hadn't been 'constantly monitoring' him, he added, he was sure he would have got one already.

McWilliams reluctantly concluded that Todino wasn't trying to sell anything or to harvest email addresses. Nor was he the front man for a book or movie promotion. He just *really believed* he was a stranded time traveller.

Whether spammers are greedy or insane, spam itself has become an unpleasant fact of life for Internet users. It doesn't seem it will ever go away, and even the best filtering programs can't eliminate all of it. So we spend a few minutes every day deleting it, and then get on with our lives. Or we try to. Some people find themselves overwhelmed by the constant, incessant barrage of junk messages, resulting in a new psychiatric condition: 'spam rage' – defined as the uncontrollable anger that builds up when a person is exposed to excessive amounts of spam.

Casual use of the term dates to 1996, but it was first used as a legal defence in 2003 when Charles Booher offered it as his excuse for leaving messages on a Canadian firm's answering machine threatening to remove the genitals of its employees using 'crude gardening tools' if they didn't stop spamming him. Booher believed the Canadian firm had sent him massive amounts of email promising to help him enlarge his penis, thereby triggering unhappy memories of his long fight against testicular cancer. Despite requests to stop, the spam persisted, until Booher flipped out and went on the offensive.

For his actions Booher faced five years in prison and a $250,000 fine. His lawyer anticipated an out-of-court resolution to the case. After all, what jury would side with the penis-enhancement spammers? And in fact, many people on the Internet regarded Booher as a hero. But after he was charged with the crime, his personal life spiralled downhill. Depressed and out of work (no one would hire him once they googled his name), he took his life a week before the trial. In doing so, he became the web's first spam martyr.

REALITY RULE 7.2
Don't forward that email!

According to biologists, any entity that reproduces or creates copies of itself can be said to be alive. By this definition, one form of email might qualify as living. It tricks people into believing that they'll be doing a good deed if they forward it. In reality, forwarding it only helps the email create more and more copies of itself, each then spawning more copies until the original has propagated throughout the Internet. It is known informally as the Email Forward Hoax, and it should be ruthlessly stamped out whenever encountered.

Identifying Email Forward Hoaxes is not difficult. They almost always contain some variation of the line: *Forward this to everyone you know*. The problem is that even when you've seen thousands of the things, you may wind up thinking, 'This one sounds legitimate.' So you click the forward button, and off the email goes to ensnare another victim.

The Email Forward Hoax comes in four varieties. Anything that looks in any way, shape, or form like one of these should be purged from your inbox. When in doubt, delete.

#1. The Petition. It claims that something bad is happening, and to stop it you need to add your name to a petition at the bottom of the email. Then you need to forward the petition to everyone you know. The bad thing could be the Brazilian rainforest being chopped down, funding for public radio being slashed, or deviants growing bonsai kittens in glass jars. It doesn't really matter.

The reality is that adding your name to an email petition won't do anything to stop the problem, because politicians don't pay any attention to such petitions. Also, the problem it addresses is probably either not real or inaccurately described. Forward the petition to your trash can.

#2. Email Tracing. You're told that a large corporation will pay you to forward their email to all your friends. This corporation supposedly has advanced technology that allows it to trace emails, so they'll know how many times you've forwarded their message, and they'll reward you accordingly.

The reality is that no one is going to pay you to forward an email, and no company has the ability to trace email remotely. Some versions of this hoax promise you'll get a gift certificate at restaurants such as Outback Steakhouse or Starbucks, or that you'll get a free flight on British Airways. Other versions state large corporations such as AOL or Nike will pay you cash. The original version, from which all the many variations derive, claimed to be a message from Bill Gates that read:

> My name is Bill Gates. I have just written up an email-tracing program that traces everyone to whom this message is forwarded to. I am experimenting with this and I need your help. Forward this to everyone you know, and if it reaches 1,000 people, everyone on the list will receive $1,000 at my expense. Enjoy. Your friend, Bill Gates.

It's rare to find the author of an email hoax, but thanks to the sleuthing of *Wired* reporter Jonathon Keats, we know that on 18 November 1997 Iowa State student Bryan Mack created the first version of this email, and sent it as a joke to a friend sitting beside him. From that innocent start, it rapidly spread throughout the Internet. If ever a situation called for the intervention of a time traveller this would be it. Mission: go back to 1997 and stop Bryan Mack from hitting the send key.

#3. The Plea for Help. This is an attempt to pull on your heartstrings. A terminally ill child, you're told, wants to collect as many business cards as possible in order to get into the *Guinness Book of World Records*. Help the kid reach his goal by sending a card and forwarding the message to all your friends.

The original version of this message (which predated the Internet) claimed that nine-year-old Craig Shergold was dying of a brain tumour and wanted to receive as many get-well cards as possible. The story was true, and Craig got millions of cards. But then he recovered and didn't want to keep getting the cards. Too late – the cards kept coming. Then email came along and the message spread even further. Somewhere along the way the plea for get-well cards became a plea for business cards, and the names of different terminally ill patients replaced Craig's. There have now been email pleas on behalf of Debbie Shwartz, Little Rachel, Baby Natalie, and many others. Sometimes the message claims a company will donate five cents to the family of the child for each forwarded message (thereby combining the Email Tracing Hoax with the Plea for Help Hoax). Donate money to medical research if you feel moved by the child's story, but trash the email.

#4. The Warning. A dangerous computer virus is spreading by email. Whatever you do, don't open it. But please, forward this warning to all your friends and co-workers to protect them.

That's the pitch, and the reality is that viruses do spread by email, which gives this hoax credibility. So maybe the warning is real, or maybe it's not. But you won't know by guessing. What you should do, instead of immediately forwarding the warning to your friends, is to check online for more information – 99 per cent of the time you'll discover the warning is bogus.

Rather than a virus, the subject of the warning might be health or crime related (watch out for poison in bottles of perfume!) or about stupid government legislation (the government wants to tax email!). Whatever the case, do your homework and resist the urge to hit forward.

However, there is one warning message you should take seriously. It refers to the Gullibility Virus. This virus, the message informs us, is spreading rapidly. It causes those infected 'to believe without question every groundless story, legend, and dire warning that shows up in their inbox or on their browser'. Symptoms of infection include, 'The willingness to believe improbable stories without thinking; the urge to forward multiple copies of such stories to others; and a lack of desire to take three minutes to check to see if a story is true.' Those who suspect they've been infected, we are told, should 'rush to their favourite search engine and look up the item tempting them to thoughtless credence.' Good advice.

REALITY RULE 7.3

Wealthy strangers are not eager to give you their money.

'Dear Friend,' the email begins, 'It is with hope that I write to seek your help in the context below.' Sounds innocent enough, but this is a typical set-up for one of the most widespread cons on the Internet, the Nigerian Bank Scam – so named because it was long a speciality of Nigerian con artists (though lowlifes throughout the world now practise it).

Once you get past the cordial introduction, what unfolds is a tale of political intrigue, shady dealings, and conspiracy. The quirky literary merits of these emails have attracted something of a cult following. As Douglas Cruickshank put it on Salon.com, Nigerian-scam buffs can't get enough of 'the characters, the earnest, alluring evocations of dark deeds and urgent needs, Lebanese mistresses, governments spun out of control, people abruptly "sacked" for "official misdemeanors" and all manner of other imaginative details all delivered in a prose style that is as awkward and archaic as it is enchanting'.

The correspondent informs you that a large sum is stuck in a foreign bank account. Maybe the money came from an inheritance. Maybe it was illegally skimmed from a legitimate business such as oil drilling. Whatever the case may be, the money needs to be moved out of the foreign country and into a place where it can be more readily accessed. That's where you come in. The correspondent wants to transfer it into your bank account. For allowing this, you'll be given 10 per cent (or more) as payment.

Should you be foolish enough to respond, you'll be asked for details about your bank account, giving the scammers access to your savings. You'll also be informed that they need you to provide some money up front to cover incidental costs involved with transferring the money: taxes, banking fees, bribes, etc. These incidentals may run to thousands or hundreds of thousands of dollars. Don't expect to see any of the money you send ever again. If you deal with these scammers long enough, you may even be lured to Nigeria (or wherever they operate), only to find yourself thrown in a cell and held for ransom. A few cases of this scam have ended in murder.

It may seem hard to believe that anyone falls for the Nigerian Bank Scam any more, but people lose millions to it every year – even highly educated people who, one would think, really should know better. Take the case of Harvard University professor Weldong Xu.

When Weldong Xu received an email informing him of a

'business proposal' that would transfer $50 million into his bank account, he thought it was the answer to his financial problems. The only catch was the usual 'unforeseen expenses' amounting to hundreds of thousands of dollars. He raised $600,000 from friends and colleagues, telling them he was collecting money to fund SARS research in China. One friend even remortgaged his house to supply Xu with cash. It all went to the scammers. Xu's charade finally came to an end when his employer became aware of his fund-raising efforts and tipped off the police. But even after he was arrested, Xu continued to insist that his friends overseas were going to send him $50 million. At his trial in 2004 his lawyer conceded that, despite being a professor, Xu was kind of a 'gullible guy'.

The prevalence of the Nigerian Bank Scam has inspired the rise of a group of amateur crime fighters who call themselves 'scambaiters'. They attempt to turn the tables on the criminals. When they receive a bank scam email, they reply to it and attempt to string the scammer along with a series of bizarre stories. If nothing else, they'll waste the scammer's time, but the ultimate goal is to see if they can actually convince him to send them money.

In 2004 the BBC reported a case in which a scambaiter named Mike convinced a Nigerian scammer that he was Father Hector Barnett of the Church of the Painted Breast. As Father Barnett, he told the scammer that he would love to do business with him, but first the scammer would have to join his church. The initiation ceremony was simple, Father Barnett assured: 'Just paint a red circle on your chest and mail me the picture.' The picture soon arrived in the mail. Next Father Barnett convinced the scammer that he also needed a 'withdrawal fee' of $80 before he could return the favour and send $80,000 in 'processing fees'. The scammer sent $80.

Unfortunately, not all criminals are so gullible.

Reality Check

Question 1. The frowny-face emoticon :-(has been trademarked, thereby making it illegal to use the symbol in emails without permission. True or false?

Question 2. A widely circulated email message warns: 'Johns Hopkins has recently sent this out in their newsletters . . . Dioxin Carcinogens cause cancer. Especially breast cancer. Don't freeze your plastic water bottles with water as this releases dioxin in the plastic.' Is the warning true or false?

Question 3. A computer virus named the Strunkenwhite Virus returns email messages that have grammatical or spelling errors. The virus 'is deadly accurate in its detection abilities, unlike the dubious spell checkers that come with word processing programs'. True or false?

Question 4. Microsoft once made a bid to buy the Catholic Church. True or false?

ANSWERS

1. It is true that the frowny-face emoticon has been registered as a trademark. In 1998 Despair.com, an online retailer of 'demotivational posters' (parodies of popular motivational posters) jokingly submitted an application to register this widely used symbol as a trademark. Two years later it

was shocked to receive notice its claim had been approved. The company promptly issued a press release warning that anyone who used the frowny symbol in an email message or online chat room without permission would face criminal prosecution. When people who didn't realize the warning was a joke flooded the company with angry emails, the company relented and announced it would sell frownies to anyone who wished to use them. Again, a joke. No one is going to sue you for using frownies, and you don't have to pay to use them either. :-)

2. Johns Hopkins never sent out a newsletter suggesting any such thing. In fact, Dr Rolf Halden of the Johns Hopkins Bloomberg School of Public Health went on record to debunk this hoax, noting that if freezing the plastic bottle were to do anything, it would probably make the water inside safer to drink because 'freezing actually works against the release of chemicals'. Heating plastic water bottles is another matter, as 'another group of chemicals that are used to make plastic less brittle can be released if you place them in hot water or heat them in the microwave'. But considering all the junk consumers willingly shove into their mouths, the 'minuscule amounts of chemical contaminants' that could get into food or water by heating plastic in the microwave shouldn't be high on anyone's list of worries.

3. False. This is an example of a spoof email warning. It was penned as a joke by journalist Bob Hirschfeld and originally appeared in his *Washington Post* column, but it subsequently circulated widely online. The name Strunkenwhite alludes to a popular writing style guide, *The Elements of Style*, by William Strunk and E. B. White.

Other examples of spoof warnings include the 'Honor

System' virus, which asks recipients, 'Please forward this message to everyone you know, then delete all the files on your hard disk. Thank you for your cooperation.'

There is also a warning that is simply titled 'Urgent Hoax Warning'. The text reads:

> I hate those hoax warnings, but this one is important! Send this warning to everyone on your email list. If someone comes to your front door saying they are conducting a survey and asks you to take your clothes off, do not do it!!! This is a scam; they only want to see you naked. I wish I'd gotten this yesterday. I feel so stupid and cheap now . . .

4. False. In 1994 a faux press release circulated widely via email, alleging that Microsoft was buying the Catholic Church. The release proclaimed, 'In a joint press conference in St. Peter's Square this morning, Microsoft Corp. and the Vatican announced that the Redmond software giant will acquire the Roman Catholic Church in exchange for an unspecified number of shares of Microsoft common stock. If the deal goes through, it will be the first time a computer software company has acquired a major world religion.' Pope John Paul II, under the terms of the deal, would have become the senior vice president of the company's new Religious Software division, and Steven Ballmer would have been invested in the College of Cardinals. Microsoft would also have gained exclusive electronic rights to the Bible. The press release may sound silly now, but at the time enough people believed it that Microsoft felt compelled to issue a statement denying it was purchasing any world religion. Soon afterwards a follow-up press release began to circulate claiming that IBM had bought the Episcopal Church.

EIGHT

eBay

All monstrosities, curiosities and knick-knacks seem to have but one purpose in this world: to be sold on eBay. During the past ten years eBay has become the one-stop shop for all the mummified alien corpses, uneaten toast, celebrity-chewed sticks of gum, discarded toenails, raccoon penis bones, Nazi pin cushions, and nudist-colony Barbie dolls that our society brings into being. Its reach extends even into the great beyond, as the retailer of choice for miracle-working tortilla chips, ghosts hidden in closets, and satanically possessed toasters. Have fun shopping there; just don't expect a guarantee of authenticity with your purchase.

REALITY RULE 8.1

A good story can sell anything.

It boggles the mind. People bid huge amounts on eBay to purchase items such as Uncle Bob's glass eye or an empty jar. The merchandise appears to be junk. Worthless. And yet it obviously has value to some people. Why?

It doesn't make sense unless you realize that it's the story about the item that interests people. Not the item itself. An old roll of toilet paper wouldn't attract much interest, but an old roll of toilet paper from the EMI Abbey Road Studios where The Beatles once recorded – that's a different matter. A good story can transform a piece of trash into a must-have item. When people bid on these items, they're often really casting a vote of appreciation for the story.

The stories can take many forms – jokes, tall tales, true-life confessions – and they often strain credulity, but this doesn't seem to deter the bidders. Three themes are particularly popular: love gone wrong, celebrity cast-offs, and the supernatural.

#1. Love Gone Wrong. In August 2008, a pair of women's underwear was put up for sale on eBay Australia. They were advertised as the 'tart's knickers' belonging to the woman a wife found her husband cheating with. Sceptics noted that the seller offered no proof that her story of returning home unexpectedly and finding a condom wrapper on the bed and women's underwear on the floor was true. Nevertheless, the underwear eventually went for $303, proving that nothing sells quite like revenge.

The classic love-gone-wrong auction took place in April 2004, when Larry Star put his ex-wife's wedding dress up for sale. That fact alone wasn't too remarkable. What made people take notice was that Star used the auction as an opportunity to launch into an extended rant about his ex-wife, her Texas cheerleader hairdo, the 'drunken sot of an ex-father-in-law' with whom he had been saddled ('Luckily I only got stuck with his daughter for 5 years. Thank the Lord we didn't have kids'), and married life in general. He also chose to model the dress himself.

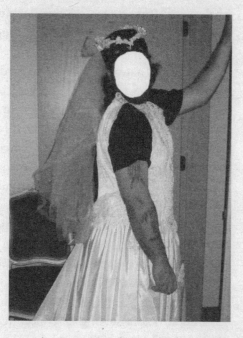

Larry Star, aka Wedding Dress Guy.

The auction attracted over fifteen million visitors and landed Star interviews on *The Today Show*, MSNBC, CNBC, as well as in *Crossdresser's Digest*. But reporters discovered that some of his story's details weren't entirely accurate. For instance, he actually had two ex-wives, neither of whom had lived with him for five years, and he did have a child with his second wife. Star shrugged off these inaccuracies as poetic license, pointing out that the central fact of his auction was correct: he did have a wedding dress for sale. The dress finally sold for $3,850, which should have netted Star a profit of $2,650, except that the winning bidder never paid up. So Star was left with the dress. As he puts it, 'I got nothing. Nada. Zilch.' But he did manage to transform the experience into a book, *Bitter, Party of One . . . Your Table is Ready: Relationship advice from a guy who has no business giving it.*

#2. Celebrity Cast-offs. It might be hard to find takers for a piece of used chewing gum, but not for a piece of gum chewed by Britney Spears. Internet entrepreneurs have realized that the detritus left behind by stars – the things they've touched, sat on, partially chewed, licked, or blown their noses with – has great value in this age of celebrity worship.

Britney's semi-masticated chewing gum debuted on eBay in August 2004. The seller claimed he had found the 'Britney Spear-Mint' in the foyer of London's Sanderson Hotel where Britney had stayed. He assured potential bidders that this was the real deal – straight from the pop star's mouth. 'Of all things, I would NOT put something on eBay that was not true,' he declared. Of course he wouldn't. Bidding topped $3 million before settling at a more reasonable $1,000. It wasn't reported if the final bidder paid up.

The auction inspired a frenzy of imitators. eBay entrepreneurs started finding Britney-chewed gum in all corners of the world: Juicy Fruit she had discarded in LA, sticks of spearmint she had flung to the pavement in Australia. Nor was the Britney fire sale limited to gum. Britney's cigarette butts went up for sale, as did corn cobs she had gnawed on, trash bags she had left behind her house in Malibu, a water bottle she had deposited on the beach in Santa Monica, and a Kleenex she had blown her nose in. Britney's spokeswoman dismissed the auctions as 'pathetic'.

Other celebrity trash put up for sale has included a cough drop sucked on by Arnold Schwarzenegger, Paris Hilton's pubic hair (supposedly found in her hotel room), Justin Timberlake's half-eaten French toast (plate included), and water Elvis Presley once sipped from. (Just the water – the cup wasn't included.)

The rage for items touched or mouthed by celebrities has even spawned a secondary market in items that have *not* been in the presence of anyone famous. Thus we find auctions for French toast *not* eaten by Justin Timberlake and gum *not* chewed by Britney Spears.

#3. The Supernatural. Two kinds of supernatural items are popular on eBay: the sacred and the spooky. Both are equally dubious.

The most famous auction of a pseudo-sacred item on eBay was the Virgin Mary Grilled Cheese Sandwich (VMGCS). Diana Duyser put this up for sale in 2004. She wrote that it was a sandwich she had cooked ten years earlier. She had taken one bite before noticing, in her words, 'a face looking up at me; it was Virgin Mary staring back at me. I was in total shock.' For the next ten years Duyser kept the sandwich in a plastic box on her night stand, where it miraculously resisted mould and disintegration (or not so miraculously considering what American cheese is made of) and brought 'blessings' to her. For instance, she attributed a big win in a casino to its divine influence. But eventually she was ready to pass the blessings on to someone else . . . for the right price.

Sceptics asked the usual questions. How did Duyser know the face was that of the Virgin Mary? What proof did she have that the sandwich was ten years old? But such questions were brushed aside by believers in the ensuing frenzy to own this rare religious artefact. It eventually sold for $28,000 to the online casino goldenpalace.com, a company that knew a good publicity opportunity when it saw one.

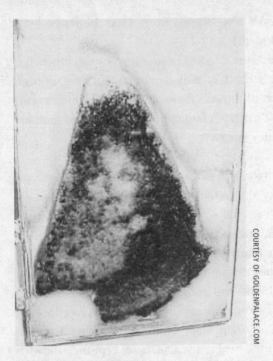

The Virgin Mary Grilled Cheese Sandwich

Following the auction of the VMGCS, the sale of food bearing the likeness of deities took off. eBay hosted auctions of deity-themed frozen fish sticks, M&Ms, popcorn, pretzels, Doritos, and much, much more. And, of course, there were also VMGCS spin-offs: an automatic Virgin Mary grilled cheese sandwich maker, numerous sandwiches that did *not* bear the image of the Holy Mother, VMGCS clocks, T-shirts, watercolour prints, and even the 'VMGCS original motion-picture soundtrack' recorded by a band in New York. The success of the VMGCS inspired Duyser to auction off the frying pan in which she had cooked it. goldenpalace.com scooped this up as well for the bargain price of $5,999.

Which means that the online casino owns both the holy sandwich and the holy frying pan. Lunch, anyone?

In the pseudo-spooky category, a standout was the 'ghost in a jar'. TJ offered this for sale in May 2003. His story was that he had been snooping around a cemetery with his metal detector when he sensed something in the ground. Upon digging down, he discovered two glass jars and a journal. As he took the jars out of the ground, one broke and released an eerie black mist. TJ left the broken jar behind and took the journal and the intact jar to his house, but the black mist followed its companion in the remaining glass jar. When TJ got into bed that night the mist attacked him, pinning him down momentarily before he escaped its grasp. From that point on, the mist was never far away, attacking him two more times in the next weeks and appearing menacingly

The ghost in a jar.

around the house. So TJ did what any one of us in his situation would do. He auctioned the jar and journal on eBay.

The ghost in a jar was an instant hit. Fan clubs appeared online, and bids reached a staggering $100 million, at which point eBay decided the bids were hoaxes and restarted the auction. The jar-bound ghost was promptly bid back up to $50,000 before the auction was closed. Unfortunately for TJ the new winning bid was also a hoax, which means, one assumes, he's still saddled with the ghost in a jar.

Although TJ wasn't able to get rid of his spooky container, his auction did inspire numerous copycat sales. February 2004 saw the auction of a 'satanic toaster' that maliciously burnt toast and refused to be thrown away. (It repeatedly found its way back from the dumpster.) Someone else offered a haunted rubber ducky. And a few months later there was a 'ghost in a Coke can', the ghost's presence being evidenced by the fact that the can had 'opened itself'. The trend descended into farce (assuming it hadn't started there) when the owner of the haunted Coke can openly admitted his item was a joke, which nevertheless didn't stop it from receiving copious amounts of media attention. Today items such as 'haunted Gmail accounts' or 'haunted potato chips' still can be yours. They're all just a mouse-click away.

Reality Check

Question 1. Gift cards often sell on eBay for more than their face value. True or false?

Question 2. A man fetched £1,550 on eBay for a Brussels sprout left over from his Christmas dinner. True or false?

1. Strange, but true. At first glance, paying more than face value for a gift card would seem absurd, like paying two dollars to get one dollar, and yet it is common to find gift cards selling for more than face value on eBay. There are several reasons why this happens. First, the buyers may have coupons giving them a percentage off any eBay purchase. The coupon makes it profitable for them to pay more than the face value of the card. Second, if the seller offers free shipping, it might be more of a bargain to pay above face value rather than buy the card from the store's website that doesn't offer free shipping (or even to drive to the store). Gift cards are popular items on eBay, but if you decide to buy one it's important to examine the reputation of the seller, because there's a lot of fraud in gift-card resale. Scam artists often sell cards they don't have, or sell the same card multiple times.

2. In January 2006 a leftover Brussels sprout, named Nicholas, did sell on eBay for £1,550. Leigh Knight, a heating parts specialist from Stockton, put it up for sale. Bidders were not entirely crazy, however. Proceeds from the sale went to Cancer Research. Knight turned down an offer to swap his sprout for a carrot.

NINE

Technology

Modern society has given rise to two distinct kinds of people: Luddites and Techno-Utopians. Luddites take their name from a group of nineteenth-century workers who attacked new textile machinery because they feared technology as a dehumanizing force. Their modern-day descendants are the kind of people who refuse to get a mobile phone and still don't use email. Techno-Utopians, on the other hand, love technology. They can't wait for each new gadget to come out and honestly believe the Internet will usher in a golden age of peace and harmony. Both groups suffer from their fair share of delusions.

REALITY RULE 9.1

The World of Tomorrow is always five to ten years away.

According to the popular science magazines of the mid-twentieth century, a techno-utopia was just around the corner. It would be a world of abundant nuclear energy and atomic-powered cars. Plus, we were all going to have robot butlers and personal jet packs. It hasn't quite turned out that way.

The predictions of a techno-utopia may not have come true, but the science magazines of today are no less optimistic. It's hard to open one without coming across breathless reports of discoveries in alternative-energy research that are going to end the world's reliance on oil within five to ten years. That always seems to be the time horizon for the utopian World of Tomorrow. Five to ten years. The phrase is the scientific equivalent of, 'The cheque is in the post.'

Because of the constant disappointment of failed predictions, there's been a steady growth of an anticipatory form of backlash known as 'forelash syndrome', characterized by cynicism about heavily hyped technologies of the future. Those who suffer from this condition are known to roll their eyes dismissively at any mention of the world-changing potential of nanotechnology, genetic engineering, or quantum computing.

Still, the hard-core techno-enthusiasts don't give up hope. They spend hours fantasizing about the cool new stuff engineers are designing, and they crowd technology conventions to be the first to witness whatever new product Apple or Microsoft is offering. Their eagerness to believe provides a ready audience for a time-honoured swindle – the Phoney Invention Scam.

The way this swindle works is that an inventor appears who claims to have developed an amazing new technology. Never mind that his invention defies the known laws of physics. He convinces investors that this is the Next Big Thing in technology, and they shower him with money. Only later do they discover that the only thing he ever invented was a pack of lies.

Back in the nineteenth century, John Worrell Keely successfully worked this scam by claiming to have invented a 'vibratory generator' capable of producing enough power – using only a quart of water as fuel – to run a train for over an hour. He just needed a little more time to perfect it. In five to ten years, he assured investors, it would be ready for commercial use, and everyone who had backed him would be a millionaire! Ultimately he strung his investors along for fourteen years, and then he died, leaving nothing but a roomful of empty promises.

In 1897 the Reverend P. F. Jernegan attracted attention by demonstrating a machine that could suck gold out of sea water. He called it the Gold Accumulator. He demonstrated it in Narragansett Bay, lowering it into the water and letting it run overnight. When pulled up in the morning, it was full of the precious metal. Businessmen rushed to invest in his company, the Electrolytic Marine Salts Company. Only when he absconded to Europe with all the money did the investors discover that the reason the machine had been able to suck gold out of the sea was because Jernegan's accomplice, a trained diver, had swum underwater and filled it with gold.

More recently, Czech businessman Sheldon Zelitt claimed to have invented 'GroutFree' technology that could seamlessly join multiple LCD screens into one large screen. This promised to offer a cheap way to mass-produce large-screen TVs. He said he was developing this product at his company in Canada, VisuaLabs. Based on this promise, the company achieved a valuation of over $300 million, but when Zelitt finally gave a demonstration of the product, a few of his investors realized that what he was showing them was simply a 42-inch plasma television available at any consumer electronics retailer. Faced with criminal charges, Zelitt fled to the Czech Republic. He was extradited back to Canada in 2005, where he's now serving an eight-year sentence.

The Vaporware Tease is a distant cousin of the non-existant product scam, though perhaps it is too harsh to describe it as a scam. Rather, it's an example of hyped expectations colliding with reality. Here a manufacturer announces a shipping date for a highly anticipated new product. Consumers patiently wait, but when the shipping date arrives, there's no product – only a new shipping date further in the future. This cycle goes on and on, ad infinitum. Unlike the non-existent product scam, the manufacturer actually has a real product in their workshop, but, to put it charitably, they're overly optimistic about its state of readiness.

The classic example of vaporware is the video game *Duke Nukem Forever*. In 1997, 3D Realms announced it would soon release this game, which was to be a follow-up to its popular title *Duke Nukem*. Twelve years later, fans are still waiting. In 2003 *Wired* magazine gave *Duke Nukem Forever* a 'lifetime achievement' award on its annually updated list of the top vaporware products. Impatient fans have taken to calling the sequel *Duke Nukem Whenever* or *Duke Nukem Taking Forever*. One *Wired* reader pointed out, 'NASA has planned, designed, developed and successfully landed a rover on Mars in the time this game has been in development.' At this point, people are rooting for the game *not* to be released. They don't want to see it break its vaporware record.

REALITY RULE 9.2

The more widely adopted a technology becomes, the more it is distrusted.

On the opposite end of the spectrum from the technophiles, we find the technophobes. This species is convinced that our modern technological conveniences are slowly crippling and killing us. TVs are turning our brains into mush. Microwave ovens are making our food toxic. The Internet is creating a generation of antisocial zombies. The list goes on and on.

Sociologists refer to the emergence of rumours about the dangers of new forms of technology as the Gremlin Effect. The term derives from World War II legends about mischievous creatures to whom technological failures were attributed. Whenever an airplane's engine mysteriously failed to start, or a car would stall, engineers would nod their heads and say, 'It must be the Gremlins again.' A widely cited example of the Gremlin Effect is a story that circulated during the 1980s as sunlamps were growing in popularity. According to this rumour, there was a young woman who cooked her internal organs by visiting a tanning salon too often. There was no truth to the tale, but it nevertheless deterred many people from using sunlamps – which may not have been a bad thing, though for different reasons!

A high point of technophobia occurred in the run-up to the year 2000. Computer experts predicted that the calendar change from 1999 to 2000 would wreak havoc with the software that operated most computers, since the software had not been designed to recognize the year 2000. Scaremongers predicted a global technological meltdown that would hurl society back into a new Stone Age. Billions were spent to address the problem, but either the preventative measures were effective or the problem never had been as bad as technophobes feared, because when the ball dropped on midnight of 31 December 1999, modern civilization didn't come to an end. Computers continued to quietly work as well as they had before.

Technophobes spy possible dangers in the most seemingly innocent of technologies. For instance, they latched onto the results of a 2005 study that found that reading your email could cause a drop in IQ 'more than twice that found in marijuana smokers'. The threat to global intelligence levels made dramatic headlines, but a closer examination of the report revealed that people weren't suffering any long-term loss of intelligence. What the test actually found was that people scored worse when taking IQ tests if they were simultaneously answering email and phone calls, which is hardly surprising or alarming.

However, the true focus of obsession for technophobes is the mobile phone. Within the past two decades these devices have become almost ubiquitous, but simultaneously many have become convinced of their ability to kill, maim, or otherwise harm us in a variety of ways.

A widespread rumour is that mobile phones can blow up gas stations by generating sparks that ignite gasoline vapours. Alarmed by this possibility, in 2005 one Connecticut state senator introduced legislation that would impose a $250 fine on anyone using a mobile phone while pumping gas. But there's actually never been a recorded incident of a mobile phone causing a gas station fire. Static discharge from your own body is far more likely to ignite the gasoline vapours.

Another rumoured threat from mobile phones is their ability to attract lightning. In 2004 the *China Daily* reported that fifteen tourists were injured at the Great Wall when an elderly man transformed his phone into a lightning rod by turning it on during a storm. While mobile phones do produce ionizing radiation, which could, in high enough levels, attract lightning, the amounts they produce are negligible.

The US National Weather Service actually urges people to use mobile phones rather than landlines during storms.

A third threat: mobile phones might cause brain cancer. In fairness to the technophobes, the jury is still out on this one. There may be some truth to this concern. Medical studies haven't found a short-term correlation between mobile phone use and brain cancer, but a long-term link is harder to disprove. If you use your phone all the time, you might want to invest in a hands-free kit. And for those really worried about this danger, companies sell radiation-shielding hats and scarves, though one would think it would be easier and cheaper simply to not use a mobile phone if you're that worried about brain cancer.

Nowhere has fear of mobile phones been taken to a more bizarre extreme than in Nigeria, where in 2004 Agence France Presse reported that a panic was sweeping through the population based on the belief that receiving a phone call from one of two numbers, 0802 311 1999 or 0802 222 5999, would cause instant death. How the phones caused this loss of life was unexplained. The AFP reporter braved death and called both numbers but was unable to reach anyone. The Nigerian phone company made an announcement assuring the public that, 'from an engineering point of view, it is absolutely impracticable, and there is no such record what-soever anywhere in the world, that anyone has died or can die from merely receiving or making a phone call'. But these logical assurances did little to stem the panic.

Sadly, this list doesn't come close to exhausting the ways mobile phones might kill you. There's also the threat from drivers chatting on their phones, or the rumoured possibility of mobile phone signals interfering with life-support systems.

But these cases involve other people using mobile phones, and there's not much you can do to guard against that – unless you move to a desert island where phones are banned. Even then, watch out for the palm trees. They may be radiation-emitting mobile phone transmission towers in disguise.

Of course, technophobes worry that the insidious threat of mobile phones goes beyond a mere loss of life. The technology appears to have a corrosive effect on our moral nature as well. Specifically, researchers suggest that mobile phones turn people into liars. A 2004 Cornell University study conducted by Jeff Hancock found that telephones, in general, are the most liar-friendly form of communications technology. Hancock asked people to record where and when they told lies during a typical week, and he found that 37 per cent of lies occurred during telephone conversations. This compared with 27 per cent during face-to-face interaction, 21 per cent while instant messaging, and only 14 per cent in email. Hancock speculated that the telephone is so liar-friendly because, first, it allows real-time conversations (most lies are told on the spur of the moment); second, telephone calls, unlike emails, aren't recorded (people are reluctant to create a permanent record of their lies); and third, the detachment between the two parties during phone conversations (the liar's face can't be seen) promotes untruth.

However, mobile phones appear to bring out the liar in people far more than landlines do. James Katz, a professor of communication at Rutgers University, found that an astonishingly high number of people fake calls on mobile phones. They do this for a variety of reasons: to avoid talking to someone nearby, to make themselves look important, or to make themselves look busier than they are. In other words, people you see chatting loudly on the street may be talking to dead air. Twenty-seven of the twenty-nine students in Katz's class admitted they had faked a call. 'People are turning the technology on its head,' the *New York Times* quoted Katz as saying. 'They are taking a device that was designed to talk to people who are far away and using it to communicate with people who are directly around them.'

There are even applications for mobile phones that facilitate their use for lying. SounderCover, marketed by Simeda, adds fake background noise to a call. 'Traffic jam' can be used to convince your boss you're stuck on the road while you're actually lounging in bed. Other pre-recorded noises include 'at the dentist', 'in the park', and 'caught in a thunderstorm'.

Perhaps in an effort to counter all these negative rumours about mobile phones, technophiles have proposed a bizarre theory of their own, suggesting that mobile phones are actually good for your brain. This theory, recently articulated by David Butler, head of the National Confederation of Parent Teacher Associations in Britain, suggests that phones held next to your head act like little radiators and that the 'heating effect actually improves the neuron transfers between neural pathways, and therefore your thinking ability goes up'. Experts, however, have dismissed this theory as wishful thinking. After all, if it were true, half the teenagers in Europe and America would by now be approaching genius levels of intelligence.

Question 1. *Popular Science* magazine published this image in 1954, predicting it was what a home computer would look like in the year 2004. True or false?

Question 2. There is software that will keep pesky bugs and flying insects away from your computer as you work. True or false?

Question 3. Engineers have invented a mobile phone that can be implanted in a tooth, vibrating to notify the user of an incoming call. True or false?

Question 4. In 2003 Microsoft unveiled the iLoo, a computer system installed inside a portable toilet. True or false?

Question 5. Sony Ericsson sells a mobile phone that has a reversed keypad layout to make it easier for left-handed people to use. True or false?

Question 6. Certain models of Nokia mobile phones have built-in radar detectors that can be activated by dialling a secret code. True or false?

ANSWERS

1. In 1954 computers really were this size, so if someone had tried to imagine what a home computer would look like fifty years in the future, they might have dreamed up such a monstrosity (including the steering wheel). However, *Popular Science* never published such a picture. The photo was created in 2004 by Danish software sales and support technician Troels Eklund Andersen as an entry in a Fark Photoshop contest. (Fark is a popular weird news website – its Photoshop contests challenge 'Farkers' to digitally alter images in amusing ways.) Andersen took a photo of a submarine-manoeuvring-room exhibit at the Smithsonian, made it black and white, and pasted in the teletype-printer, the old-style television, and the man. Then he added the text at the bottom. The image began to circulate via email, becoming one of the most forwarded email attachments of 2004, and fooled thousands of people. It apparently even fooled Scott McNealy, CEO of Sun Microsystems, who displayed it at a computer conference as proof of the impossibility of predicting future technology.

2. Thai computer programmer Saranyou Punyaratanabunbhu wanted to help computer users work without fear of bug-borne malaria, which is a major problem in Thailand. So he developed software that makes computer speakers emit high-pitched frequencies inaudible to the human ear but annoying to mosquitoes. The software was downloaded 50,000 times in the first three days after it debuted, and Saranyou soon came out with a version 2.0 that also repels cockroaches and rats. A South Korean phone company, SK Telecom, now offers anti-mosquito software for mobile phones. So the software does exist. The more relevant question is whether it works. Probably not. Pest control experts at the University of Nebraska-Lincoln note, 'There is no scientific evidence to suggest that cockroaches (or any other insects) respond negatively to ultrasonic sound waves.' Even if it did work, there's one more thing to consider before installing it on your PC. Some users report getting headaches after sitting for hours in front of a computer emitting a high-pitched whine.

3. James Auger and Jimmy Loizeau, research associates at MIT Media Lab Europe, designed an audio tooth implant for the Royal College of Art's Summer 2002 exhibit. It vibrates when there's an incoming call. The user then speaks normally, and a tiny microphone picks up her voice. Incoming sounds are transferred to the inner ear via bone resonance. Unfortunately, calls can only be received, as there's no way to dial a number. The phone was an art project, so it's not available for purchase. But Auger and Loizeau stress that the technology to produce such a phone does exist.

4. On 30 April 2003, as part of Microsoft's goal to allow people to log on 'anytime, any place, and anywhere', MSN UK, a division of Microsoft, announced the imminent introduction of the iLoo, the world's first Internet-enabled port-a-potty. The iLoo was said to include a wireless keyboard, a height-adjustable flat plasma screen, a six-channel surround-sound speaker system installed under the sink, broadband Internet access, toilet paper conveniently printed with URL suggestions, and (last but not least) a toilet outfitted with vacuum suction to guarantee maximum hygiene. The media was incredulous, and peppered the corporation with questions. For instance, how were they planning to keep the thing clean? Microsoft eventually conceded that while the project *had been* under serious development in the UK, 'corporate headquarters in Redmond, Washington, looked at it and decided maybe this wasn't a good idea'.

5.   False. Virgin Mobile announced the availability of the left-handed Sony Ericsson LH-Z200 mobile phone on 31 March 2004. Online technology blogs such as Engadget and Mobile-Mag immediately wrote it up, only to be informed that it was an early April Fool's Day joke. Left-handed products are a favourite 1 April gag. In 1996 Mars Inc. ran a half-page ad in the *Daily Telegraph* announcing it would be introducing left- and right-handed versions of its signature candy bar, explaining that for years left-handed people had been opening the wrapper from the wrong end and consequently were 'eating against the chocolate flow on the bar surface'. Another famous left-handed product was Burger King's left-handed Whopper (all the condiments were rotated 180 degrees), which debuted on 1 April 1998.

6.   False. According to a popular email rumour, bored engineers designed most Nokia mobile phones to pick up radar speed traps. To activate this secret function you enter menu mode, then select (in the following order) 'settings', 'security settings', 'closed user group', and 'on'. Finally, enter 00000 and hit ok. A radar sign should appear on the screen. This series of steps has been tested on numerous Nokia phones, but not one has ever revealed the secret radar-trap-detection mode.

TEN

The News

According to legend, Sir Richard Phillips, founder of the *Leicester Herald*, was working late one night in 1792 when he accidentally knocked a column of type off a table. Lacking time to redo his work, he scooped up the scattered type, shoved it randomly into the column, and printed it out – accompanied by a note to his readers explaining that the 'Dutch mail' had arrived too late to be translated. Reportedly one reader held on to this Dutch mail edition for thirty years, hoping one day to find someone who could translate it. And so began the media's love affair with truth.

REALITY RULE 10.1

Information is only as good as its source.

The rule that 'information is only as good as its source' is the prime commandment of hoax-busting. All other rules are secondary to it. Every form of information – whether it's a photograph, a scientific discovery, or something you read in a college textbook – *always* has a source. And if that source is unreliable, so is the information. The problem is that it's often very difficult to know just how reliable a source really is. After all, even your own eyes can play tricks on you.

The news industry, in general, is a good source of information. Journalists pride themselves on being accurate and fair. But as with any profession, there are bad apples. Sometimes reporters turn rogue, and when they do they invent news out of thin air.

Once upon a time, news editors openly encouraged their reporters to be slightly roguish. Anything to spice up a slow news day. Throughout the nineteenth century newspapers were filled with hoaxes, such as the 1835 moon hoax in which the *New York Sun* convinced much of the population of America that astronomers had discovered a race of fire-wielding biped beavers living on the moon. During the time of yellow journalism (around the beginning of the twentieth century) many papers even employed 'rewrite men' whose job it was to enliven stories by adding entertaining, usually fictitious, details.

It wasn't until 1924, when *Herald Tribune* reporter Sanford Jarrell concocted a tale about a floating speakeasy anchored in international waters just outside New York harbour – causing harbour police to embark on a frantic search for the phantom 'sin ship' – that a reporter got fired for lying. Unfortunately for Jarrell, he perpetrated his hoax just as the news industry had decided it was good for business to convince readers that it adhered to a code of ethics. Of course, editors still pressured their reporters to produce plenty of sensational stories. This created a tension. On the one hand, editors told their reporters to be honest. On the other, they pushed them to come up with stories that would sell a lot of copy. Inevitably a few reporters decided to make their job easier by fabricating events. So the noisy firing of rogue reporters (while editors expressed shock that one of their staff would do such a thing) became a recurring feature in the world of journalism.

Notorious examples of rogue reporters include Bob Patterson, who in 1972 filed a series of groundbreaking reports for the *San Francisco Examiner* about his secret odyssey through Red China. These reports were made all the more remarkable when it was learned Patterson had never left his hotel in Hong Kong. In 1981 Janet Cooke won a Pulitzer Prize for her *Washington Post* articles about an eight-year-old heroin addict named Jimmy, but had to return the Pulitzer when her editors discovered that Jimmy didn't exist. Her argument that someone like Jimmy theoretically could have existed given the drug problem in Washington, DC didn't win her much sympathy, especially from the police who had been frantically searching for the boy.

During the late 1990s, Stephen Glass was a young writer on the fast track for success at the *New Republic*. He always seemed to get the scoops. His most celebrated article, 'Hack Heaven', told the story of a fifteen-year-old hacker who broke into the computer systems of Jukt Micronics and then extorted money (and a job, a Miata, a trip to Disney World, and a lifetime subscription to *Playboy*) from the software corporation. The article captured the topsy-turvy culture of the dot-com boom, but the *New Republic* fired Glass when they found out Jukt Micronics only existed in his imagination.

Finally, there was *New York Times* reporter Jayson Blair, who travelled the country, diligently doing research and conducting interviews. Or so he claimed. In reality, he spent most of his time in a New York City Starbucks sipping coffee and lifting details from other journalists' work. For which reason, he was shown the door in 2003.

Of course, not all hoaxes in the media are the fault of rogue reporters. In many cases, reporters fail to accurately judge the reliability of their sources and get taken in by hoaxes. The history of journalism is full of spectacular goofs.

In 1856 the London *Times* sparked a transatlantic row by publishing a letter describing a series of duels fought with 'Monte Christo pistols' on a Georgia train while passengers ignored the bloodshed. The paper offered this as proof of the barbaric nature of American society. The *New York Times* angrily denied that such duels had ever occurred, and the London *Times* realized it had been duped when it learned that 'Monte Christo pistols' was Southern slang for bottles of champagne.

Perhaps the most famous case of the media being hoaxed is 1983's Hitler diaries fiasco. The German magazine *Der Stern* thought it had scored a journalistic coup when it obtained the secret diaries of Adolf Hitler, supposedly hidden in East Germany since the end of World War II. The magazine wanted so badly for the diaries to be real that it ignored obvious evidence to the contrary, such as Hitler's well-known dislike of keeping personal records. *Der Stern* only admitted the diaries weren't real, and were actually the work of a forger named Konrad Kujau, after it became clear they were written on paper manufactured long after the war's end, and that their content had been lifted from an edition of *Hitler's Speeches and Proclamations*. All told, the debacle cost the magazine upward of $24 million.

A lesser known, but more peculiar example of the media being hoaxed involved the 'man on the street' interviews that reporters love to conduct. In such interviews, a reporter swoops down on a random pedestrian to quiz him about the latest headlines. In 2003, media critics noticed that the same man kept popping up time after time in 'man on the street' interviews. Greg Packer, a highway maintenance worker from upstate New York, was quoted by the *New York Times*, the *New York Daily News*, the *Los Angeles Times*, the *New York Post*, the *Philadelphia Inquirer*, the London *Times*, and other publications. He also appeared on CNN, MSNBC, and Fox. But he was always described as nobody special, just a random person. How had he become the go-to guy when the media needed a 'man on the street'?

It turned out that Packer was a man with a curious hobby. He camped out to be first in line at celebrity events. When the media arrived to cover the event, he was front and centre, ready to answer questions should a reporter want to talk to a fan. Often Packer waved at reporters to urge them over. Not realizing he was a serial front-of-the-line guy, the reporters happily interviewed him – again and again and again.

It helped that Packer was expert at delivering upbeat platitudes that journalists could easily use to pad an article without rocking any boats. Take, for instance, his opinion on President Clinton: 'He made his mistakes, like everybody else.' Or on the US invasion of Iraq: 'We had to do whatever we had to do.' Or on whether he preferred the Mets or the Yankees: 'I'm for both teams . . . I'm a New York fan.'

Packer was interviewed well over one hundred times before the media realized what was going on. When the story of his ubiquity broke, the *New York Daily News* dubbed him the 'most quoted Everyman in the country'. The Associated Press distributed a memo urging its reporters not to quote Packer any more, but the news organization refused to say it would never again run his name. It noted the possibility that he might one day actually do something newsworthy.

Truth is often stranger than fiction, but that doesn't mean every strange thing is true.

In June 2002 the *Beijing Evening News* ran a story about unusual negotiations taking place between the US Congress and the district government of Washington, DC. Congress was apparently threatening to leave Washington if the city didn't pay for the construction of a new Capitol Hill building outfitted with a retractable dome. Was the story true? No. But was it a deliberate hoax? Also, no. A *Beijing Evening News* reporter had found the story on the website of *The Onion*, a satirical magazine, and neither he nor his editor had realized it was a joke – a farcical take on sports teams that pressure city governments to build them new stadiums at taxpayer expense.

As news sources proliferate (thanks to the Internet), mistaking satire for news is becoming increasingly common – and it doesn't happen only to Chinese reporters unfamiliar with the nuances of American culture. The hippo-eats-dwarf story, after which this book is named, is an example of satire mistaken as news. (See the Introduction for a description of that tale.) Another case occurred in 2001 when both cartoonist Garry Trudeau and the *Guardian* referred to a study conducted by the Lovenstein Institute of Scranton, Pennsylvania that had found George W. Bush to have the lowest IQ of any American president of the past fifty years. Both Trudeau and the *Guardian* had learned of this study in a press release forwarded to them via email. That alone should have given them pause. What they didn't know was that the original source of the information was a humour website, linkydinky.com. The Lovenstein Institute and its IQ study were just a joke.

The humour publication that holds the record for having more of its stories mistaken for real news than any other is the *Weekly World News*. Published from 1979–2007, the *Weekly World News* masqueraded as a serious tabloid, claiming that it printed 'nothing but the truth', but most of its articles were obvious jokes, such as its tales of the adventures of Bat Boy, a half-human/half-bat creature found in a cave in West Virginia. Bat Boy's fictitious adventures included leading American troops in the capture of Saddam Hussein and travelling into outer space. But some of its articles were ambiguous enough to fool people who stumbled upon them and were unaware of what kind of publication the *Weekly World News* was.

A *Weekly World News* article posted online in December 2003 reported that an unknown prankster had inserted outrageously incorrect translations into a Japanese-to-English phrase book. The Japanese phrase, 'Can you direct me to the rest room?' was translated into English as, 'May I caress your buttocks?'; 'I am very pleased to meet you,' had become, 'My friend, your breath could knock over a water buffalo.' The article claimed that, as a consequence, many Japanese tourists were being verbally, and in some cases physically, assaulted after approaching people on the street and using these phrases. Thousands of Internet users mistook this for a true story.

An article about a time-travelling trader created even more confusion. This story described the curious case of Andrew Carlssin, who over a period of two weeks had transformed an initial investment of $800 into $350 million through a series of spectacular trades. This success immediately attracted the attention of the US Securities and Exchange Commission, which charged him with insider trading. After all, how else could he have made such perfect trades? But during interrogation Carlssin pleaded innocent, attributing his prescient knowledge of stock prices to the fact that he was actually a time traveller from the year 2256. Given his amazing track record, his explanation seemed oddly credible. The story of the time-travelling stock trader spread far and wide, appearing in such august publications as the London *Times*. The SEC received so many inquiries about the case that it eventually posted a statement on its website denying it had ever brought enforcement action against such a person.

In addition to the problem of satire mistaken as news, there is the closely related phenomenon of urban legends mistaken as news. Urban legends are sensational stories repeated by people who believe they're true. Their exact origins are often decades old and unknown. Reporters are no more resistant to their premises of deadly spiders hiding under toilet seats, bar-prowling kidney thieves, or $250 cookie recipes than anyone else. We have already seen, in Chapter One, how the BBC offered up the urban legend of 'the woman who gave birth to a frog' as a legitimate news story.

In January 2002 Reuters News Service reported that a woman had activated a high-pressure vacuum flush system while using a toilet on a Scandinavian Airlines flight from Sweden to the United States. The pressure from the toilet sucked her downward until her buttocks formed a perfect, airtight seal on the seat, preventing her from standing up. Only after the plane had landed in America were ground technicians able to dislodge her. 'She was stuck there for quite a long time,' a spokesman was quoted as saying. The woman subsequently filed a complaint against the airline.

Many newspapers reprinted the article from the wire service, but the story wasn't true. Scandinavian Airlines checked its complaints and could find no record of such an incident. Eventually they figured out the source of the tale. It was one of the fictional examples used in their training manual to instruct flight crews how to deal with emergencies.

Finally, there's a category of rumours occasionally transmitted by the media – particularly the media in Africa and the Middle East – that goes beyond mere urban legends or satires, and rises into the realm of full-blown, howling-at-the-moon, pitchfork-waving, aluminium-tinfoil-hat-wearing insanity. The most famous example is the tale of the penis-melting Zionist robot combs.

In September 2003, a mass panic swept through Khartoum, the capital of Sudan, triggered by a rumour that a satanic foreigner was shaking hands with Sudanese men and thereby causing their penises to melt upwards inside their bodies. One man claimed he was at the market when a stranger approached him, handed him a comb, and asked him to comb his hair. As the local press later reported: 'When he did so, within seconds . . . he felt a strange sensation and discovered that he had lost his penis.'

Instead of debunking the rumour, the regional papers fanned the hysteria by offering hypotheses about who the satanic foreigner might be. The journalist Ja'far Abbas, a columnist for the Saudi daily *Al-Watan*, made this observation:

No doubt, this comb was a laser-controlled surgical robot that penetrates the skull [and passes] to the lower body and emasculates a man!! I wanted to tell that man who fell victim to the electronic comb: 'You jackass, how can you put a comb from a man you don't know to your head, while even relatives avoid using the same comb?!' . . . That man, who, as it is claimed, is from West Africa, is an imperialist Zionist agent that was sent to prevent our people from procreating and multiplying.

The reality is that the Sudanese rumour was not evidence of imperialist Zionist agents armed with emasculating laser-controlled robot combs. Instead, it was a manifestation of what anthropologists call a 'koro' epidemic, which is the term for a shrinking-penis panic. Strangely enough, historical records contain numerous examples of such epidemics.

James Taranto, writing for the *Wall Street Journal*, is credited with introducing American readers to the story of the Sudanese panic and inspiring the phrase 'penis-melting Zionist robot combs'. As an adjective (penis-melting-Zionist-robot-comb-like) it is to be used sparingly, reserved for only the weirdest of the weird stuff that occasionally crosses the newswires.

REALITY RULE 10.3

'News is what people want to keep hidden; everything else is publicity.'*

There's a romantic image of where news comes from – journalists pounding the pavement and burning up the phone lines looking for important stories to report, tracking down sources, leaving no stone unturned. The reality is quite a bit different, and quite a bit sadder. Up to 70 per cent

---

* Bill Moyers, *NOW*, 17 December 2004.

of the content reported by the media comes directly from public relations firms.

Here's how it works. Corporations hire PR firms (or in-house media relations staff). These PR firms then try to get journalists to report favourably on what their clients are doing, or whatever ideas their clients want promoted. PR hacks send out thousands of press releases every day and often suggest story ideas directly to reporters. Sometimes these story suggestions are sweetened by accompanying gift baskets. It becomes the job of the reporter to sift through this avalanche of corporate-produced information and decide what in it is entertaining enough to be newsworthy.

A favourite tool of PR firms is the video news release (or VNR). VNRs are publicity videos designed to look like news segments. They feature fake reporters who deliver positive commentary about the corporations who have hired them. PR firms send these VNRs to TV stations that then re-edit them to look like material the stations produced themselves. The VNR ends up seamlessly integrated into news broadcasts. Stations like the arrangement because it provides them with free content (always important in these times of ever-shrinking budgets). Most viewers never know they're watching PR-created news.

Corporations have been supplying TV stations with VNRs for years, but the practice became much more controversial when it came to light that the American government was doing the same thing. This revelation scared media critics because when corporations create fake news, it's covert advertising, but when a government does the same thing, it's covert propaganda, which is far more disturbing.

American government agencies began creating VNRs during the Clinton administration, and the practice accelerated under Bush. Hundreds of these clips appeared in news broadcasts, but the one that caught the public's attention, after it was eventually exposed, was a segment designed to promote a controversial new Medicare law. It featured a 'reporter' who cheerily helped viewers 'sort through the details' of the legislation, never mentioning that it had been widely criticized as a giveaway to pharmaceutical corporations. The clip concluded with her saying, 'In Washington, I'm Karen Ryan reporting.'

What infuriated critics was that Karen Ryan wasn't reporting. She was reading from a script prepared by the Department of Health and Human Services – a fact never mentioned when the segment aired in news programmes throughout the nation. As Ryan herself later admitted, she was a 'paid shill for the Bush administration'. The *Cleveland Plain Dealer* put it even more bluntly: 'Karen Ryan, You're a Phony.'

REALITY RULE 10.4

'Journalism is founded on the premise that reality can only be shown through other people's statements.'*

The media likes to maintain the appearance of objectivity. In an ideal world this would mean clearly identifying the source of all the information it presents to the public, noting all biases or affiliations, and challenging sources to verify their claims. But in practice, news organizations have a variety of tricks they use to surreptitiously promote one point of view, or shade how the public perceives events, without actually

---

* Chuck Klosterman, *Sex, Drugs, and Cocoa Puffs*, Simon & Schuster, 2003.

lying. Below are the top five tricks journalists use to distort the news.

#1. The Misleading Statistic. Aaron Levenstein famously remarked that statistics are like bikinis: what they reveal is suggestive, but what they conceal is vital. Journalists love statistics because they appear objective, but statistics taken out of context can be twisted to support any position. Unfortunately, this is how they're often used in the media.

For instance, an old chestnut often cited in papers in the United States is the gloomy statistic that 50 per cent of all marriages end in divorce. The statistic is popular because it's attention-grabbing. But a look beneath the surface of this famous figure reveals a more ambiguous reality. The number comes from a study by the National Center for Health Statistics that found that, in one year, there were half as many divorces as there were marriages. At first glance this would seem to suggest that half of all marriages end in divorce, but the problem with arriving at this conclusion is that it's hard to extrapolate from what happened in one year to what will happen in all marriages. Moreover, the figure doesn't acknowledge variations within the population (such as the fact that people who get married very young tend to divorce at a far higher rate than people who marry later in life).

Beneath most casually quoted statistics, there almost always lies a more complicated reality.

#2. The Phoney Trend. It is the job of the media to report the news, but in doing so its reporting must remain proportional to the frequency with which events occur in the real world. By over-reporting a phenomenon, it can greatly exaggerate its importance. For instance, if it reports *every* crime, it creates the impression of a crime wave in progress. This occurred in 2002 when several dramatic child abduction cases made headlines in America. Spurred on by the public interest in the cases, the media began to report every new abduction that occurred. The public became so alarmed by this apparent crime wave that the White House convened a special Conference on Missing, Exploited and Runaway Children to address the issue. The irony was that there was no sudden surge in abductions. Their number was actually on the decline, from 263 in 2001 to 201 in 2002.

Related to the Phoney Crime Wave is the Generalization From a Single Example, in which reporters falsely magnify a few examples into evidence of a far larger trend. For instance, in January 2008 a journalist for the *Chicago Tribune* claimed that blue seemed to be the new green. By this she meant that the colour blue was replacing green as the global symbol of environmentalism. Her evidence? Mercedes-Benz had called its new clean diesel technology BLUETEC. Readers were underwhelmed.

Critics also complain that the media focuses too much on negative stories and under-reports positive ones. The evening news is full of grim stories about bank robberies and shootings. This is called the 'if it bleeds, it leads' phenomenon, and it may give audiences an unrealistically bleak view of the world. The media counters that gory, dramatic events are legitimate stories that the public wants to know about. No one would watch the news if it was devoted to the number of planes that landed safely that day. It's only the one plane that doesn't land safely people want to know about.

#3. Unbalanced Sources. When a reporter covers a controversial topic, it's considered proper she should seek opinions from those on both sides of the issue. This only seems fair. The problem is that the two sides of a debate may be grossly unbalanced in terms of credibility. A statement by a leading scientist might be contrasted with a quotation from the head of the local Bigfoot Watchers' Club, as if both were equally deserving of attention. The result is that fringe beliefs tend to be over-represented by the media. Critics argue that peripheral groups such as global-warming deniers and creationists have been able to exploit this loophole to champion their causes. Nor is the media above ignoring mainstream opinion altogether and actively seeking out the lunatic fringe on both sides of an issue – because screaming extremists always make better TV than middle-of-the-road sorts who debate more politely.

#4. **The Favoured Source.** The opposite of unbalanced sources is the favoured source. Journalists are supposed to avoid interjecting their own opinion into the news, but there's nothing to stop them from only interviewing people with whom they agree, and so reporters often rely heavily on a few favourite sources that can be counted on to say the right things. In this way, the media can maintain the guise of objectivity while simultaneously creating the impression that there's really only one credible side to an issue.

#5. **Leading Questions.** When conducting interviews, a reporter can obtain dramatically different responses by altering the phrasing of a question. For instance, the question, 'What candidate are you planning to vote for?' is straightforward and open-ended. But a reporter could instead ask, 'Would you be willing to vote for Candidate X despite the fact he's been accused of corruption?' This question suggests an answer. After all, why would anyone want to vote for a corrupt politician? Using this tactic, reporters can often get the answers they want.

Similar to the leading question is the loaded question, which presupposes something to be true. The classic example is the question, 'Are you still beating your wife?' Whether the respondent answers yes or no, they've implicitly admitted to being a wife-beater. An oft-cited example of a loaded question occurred in May 1996 when journalist Lesley Stahl of *CBS News* asked Madeleine Albright, US Ambassador to the UN, about the effect of sanctions on Iraq. She phrased her question, 'We have heard that a half million children have died. I mean, that is more children than died in Hiroshima. And, you know, is the price worth it?' Much to her regret, Albright responded that yes, the price was worth it. She later admitted she should have challenged the presupposition that half a million children had died because of the sanctions. Instead, her response made her appear heartless and cruel.

Some might say it serves a politician right to be exposed as heartless and cruel, but then again, isn't it better to expose them with straightforward questions rather than trick ones? (Note: yes, that's a leading question!)

Reality Check

Question 1. In November 2004 American newspapers reported that Indiana Congressman John Hostettler had introduced legislation to change the name of Interstate 69 to the more 'moral sounding' Interstate 63. Was the report true or satire?

Question 2. In April 2004 European newspapers reported that EU bureaucrats had banned jelly mini-cups because these bite-sized candies were deemed a threat to public safety. Was the report true or satire?

Question 3. In 1996 the *Sun* acquired a videotape of Princess Diana frolicking in her underwear with cavalry officer James Hewitt. True or false?

Question 4. In early 2003 America's CBS News broadcast an interview with Iraqi dictator Saddam Hussein in which the network provided a voice-over translation of Hussein's responses. The American actor hired to deliver the voice-over was instructed to speak in a fake Arabic accent. True or false?

ANSWERS

1. Many newspapers (some as far afield as Belgium) did print this story as fact. But the original source of the article was the *Hoosier Gazette*, an online humour site created by Josh Whicker. The *Hoosier Gazette* article quoted Hostettler as saying, 'Every time I have been out in public with an "I-69" button on my lapel, teenagers point and snicker at it. I have had many ask me if they can have my button. I believe it is time to change the name of the highway. It is the moral thing to do.' After receiving a torrent of phone calls about the story, Hostettler's office issued a statement declaring the name-change idea absurd and assuring everyone that Congressman Hostettler was a 'fervent supporter of I-69'.

2. With this question, we enter into the realm of the Euromyth, which is mid-way between satire and urban legend. According to popular rumour, overly zealous EU bureaucrats have been responsible for all manner of absurd-ities. They have been accused of reclassifying kilts as 'womenswear', decreeing that bananas sold within Europe not be 'too excessively curved', mandating that joggers not go faster than six miles per hour in city parks in order to avoid disturbing mating squirrels, and ordering that the word 'pertannually' be removed from the EU constitution (citing it as meaningless) and replaced with the much clearer term 'insubdurience'. In reality, none of these things ever hap-pened. They're all Euromyths. Most Euromyths are false, but occasionally a few turn out to be true, making all the others seem credible. The EU ban on jelly mini-cups is such a case. Although these candies sound harmless, they have a nasty habit of lodging in children's throats. These candies had been outlawed in much of the world before the EU got around to banning them.

3. False. The *Sun* reportedly paid six figures for what it thought was such a tape. However, the tape was later revealed to be the work of an amateur filmmaker who had shot it in a London suburb using two Diana look-alikes and one fake Hewitt.

Similar media goofs include the time in 1992 when CNN almost reported that the first President Bush had died, after it received a phone call from a man claiming to be the presi-dent's heart specialist on board Air Force One. Anchorman Don Harrison interrupted the regularly scheduled broadcast to deliver the news, but, just in the nick of time, someone at CNN realized it was a hoax and the producer yelled 'Stop! Stop!' Viewers could hear shouting, but didn't know what it was all about. The caller turned out to be mentally unstable.

Also, in 1997 ABC prepared a $2 million three-part documentary about the relationship between JFK and Marilyn Monroe, alleging not only that the two had engaged in a long-time affair, but that JFK had intended to establish a trust fund for Monroe's mother in order to buy the actress's silence. ABC's proof for these spectacular claims was a series of love letters supposedly written by JFK. But just in time to scuttle the series, ABC discovered the letters had been produced on a typewriter that wasn't manufactured until after Kennedy's death. Another problem was that the addresses on the letters contained zip codes, though zip codes only came into use in 1963 – again after JFK's death.

4. True. During the build-up to the second Iraq war, CBS News scored a journalistic coup by obtaining an exclusive interview with Saddam Hussein. When *60 Minutes II* broadcast the interview, the show provided a voice-over translation of Hussein's responses, but viewers were not informed that although the translation was perfectly accurate, the voice-over's thick, Arabic accent was phoney. The voice belonged to Steve Winfield, an American actor who specializes in faking accents. CBS hired Winfield to read the translation in phoney Arabic-ese in order, the station later explained, to add realism to the broadcast.

ELEVEN

Entertainment

Once upon a time, forms of entertainment were few and simple: conversation, reading, music, and dance. Nowadays our options have expanded considerably to include movies, radio, high-definition TV, and video games. There's always something to see or do. Some fear this barrage of entertainment is eroding the barrier between reality and fantasy. Others wonder how there can be five hundred channels on TV, and nothing worth watching.

REALITY RULE 11.1
There's nothing real about reality TV.

As long as there's been TV, there's been reality TV. And as long as there's been reality TV, producers have been faking the reality portion of it.

The basic premise of the reality genre is to place people in front of a camera and record their honest, unscripted reactions to events. Audiences like the spontaneity of reality shows, and TV studios love the fact that they're cheap to make. It's a match made in heaven. But TV producers need content that will reliably entertain, and much reality is ugly and dull. Which is why producers have a habit of stepping in to goose things up a bit, either on the set or in the editing room. They can't help themselves – there's too much money involved to do otherwise.

The quiz shows popular in the 1950s were the earliest form of reality TV. Audiences loved the drama of everyday people winning or losing thousands of dollars. But a series of scandals at the decade's end revealed that corporate sponsors were fixing the games behind the scenes, picking who won and who lost.

The most notorious quiz show fraud occurred on the programme *Twenty-One*. For a while, contestant Charles Van Doren – an instructor at Columbia University and son of the Pulitzer Prize-winning poet Mark Van Doren – seemed unbeatable. Week after week he won, racking up prize money of $129,000 and becoming one of the most famous people in America, revered as the epitome of elegant, cultured genius. But Herbert Stempel, a previous contestant on the show, became jealous of Van Doren's success and revealed that he had been instructed to let Van Doren win. Not only had Van Doren been given the answers by the producers of the show, he had also been coached to draw out the tension by pretending to struggle to come up with correct answers. The *Twenty-One* scandal ended the reign of the prime-time quiz shows, but it didn't end fake reality TV.

In the 1980s daytime talk-show hosts like Oprah Winfrey, Sally Jessy Raphael, Phil Donahue, and Geraldo commanded huge audiences. Their appeal lay in the real people who would appear on their shows, brazenly confessing all manner of taboo vices and problems. Topics ranging from 'caring for disabled lesbian lovers', to 'makeovers for drag queens', to 'I'm sixteen and I'm a nymphomaniac' earned the shows the label 'Trash TV'.

Sceptics suspected at least some of the guests were fakes or actors, and the sceptics were right. In 1988 it came to light that one couple, part-time performers Tani Freiwald and Wes Bailey, had appeared on numerous talk shows by claiming to be different people suffering from different problems. On *The Oprah Winfrey Show*, Freiwald posed as Bailey's sex-hating wife. On *The Sally Jessy Raphael Show* she became a sex worker trying to cure Bailey's impotence, and on *Geraldo* she transformed herself into a sex surrogate hired to help Bailey, who now claimed to be a thirty-five-year-old virgin.

The talk shows promised to reform and better screen their guests, but ten years later a rash of fake-guest scandals in both America and England proved that things were still the same. Cases included a woman who shaved her head and pretended to have cancer in order to get on *Oprah*, and a wagonload of phoney guests – recruited from an entertainment agency – who appeared on the BBC's *Vanessa Show*.

The 1992 debut of MTV's *The Real World* launched a new phase of the reality TV phenomenon – the real-life soap operas and extreme-challenge contests phase. On *The Real World* cameras recorded the tribulations of seven young strangers living in a New York City apartment. This was followed a few years later by the success, in both Europe and America, of *Survivor*, a show about 'castaways' who had to survive on a desert island while voting a fellow contestant off the island each week.

This new form of reality programming spread across the airwaves like a fungus, but claims of fakery plagued almost all the major shows. On *Survivor* there were accusations that votes had been rigged, shots staged, and cast members hired through modelling agencies. It was reported that Ozzy Osbourne's teenage children claimed certain scenes in *The Osbournes* were staged for dramatic effect.

With audiences growing more cynical about the reality of reality TV, studios began to design shows that were openly dishonest. In this vein Fox debuted *Joe Millionaire*, on which women competed for the affections of a man they thought was a millionaire, only to learn at the end of the series that he was a '$19,000-a-year construction worker'. But even here not all was as it seemed. Critics pointed out that Fox's faux millionaire was a swimsuit model as well as a construction worker and earned far more than $19,000 a year. There were even rumours that he really was a millionaire.

Even less sensational reality fare has been rocked by scandal. The American version of *Antiques Roadshow* seemed about as homey and non-controversial as a programme could get. It featured professional antiques dealers appraising people's collectibles and family heirlooms. The fun part was when people discovered things they thought were junk were worth thousands of dollars. But in March 2000 the public learned that a number of appraisals had been staged. Most notorious was an episode in which a man brought in a sword he said had been lying around his attic. He didn't think it was worth anything, so he had been using it to cut watermelons. The dealer then told him it was a rare Confederate sword valued at tens of thousands of dollars. Courtroom confessions later revealed that the appraisal was scripted in advance. The dealer and owner had invented the entire story, including the part about cutting watermelons. The sword, however, was real.

Shows that feature bloopers, out takes, and amusing scenes caught on video have long been a TV staple. But as with everything else in the world of reality programming, many of the spills and slip-ups aren't bloopers at all, but carefully choreographed fakes. Fox's *Stupid Behavior Caught on Tape* showed an aerobics instructor getting hopelessly tangled in a skipping rope, but reporters who saw the original tape could hear an offstage director shouting directions. *Caught on Tape!* captured the world's worst employees: a pizza chef casually serving customers food he'd dropped on the floor, a hapless sandwich maker, and an unhygienic delivery man. A closer look revealed that all three employees were the same man, who happened to be the video's producer. According to a report that aired on Bravo, *The Reality of Reality: How Real Is Real?*, as many as 75 per cent of the bloopers collected by the clip-show business are fake.

Even documentaries are not always as real as they claim to be. British documentaries, in particular, have been prone to fakery in recent years. *The Connection* was a Carlton Television documentary about Colombian drug smugglers. But after parts of it aired in the US on CBS's *60 Minutes* in 1998, it was exposed as a near-total fake. The Colombians were actors, the heroin was sugar, and the central character – a mole hired to smuggle drugs on flights from Colombia to Britain – was a car-park attendant who never smuggled anything. Then there was *Daddy's Girl*, a Channel 4 film about incestuous fathers and daughters. It had to be scrapped when the featured father and daughter were revealed to be unrelated. Channel 4 was also censured for *Chickens*, about the lives of Glasgow 'rent boys' (male prostitutes). The production team admitted it had staged scenes showing the rent boys negotiating with clients.

Nature documentaries may be the most egregious offenders, simply because they seem above reproach. How could footage of mating polar bears be faked? But in a 2004 article, Sir David Attenborough revealed some of the tricks of the trade. Mating polar bears, for instance, would likely be filmed in a zoo, with footage spliced in to make it appear the bears were in the wild. Or a dramatic scene of a falcon catching its prey could be faked by filming three independent shots: one of the bird's prey, a second of the bird swooping downwards, and a final shot of feathers flying into the air (tossed up by a member of the film crew). These shots would then be combined to form one scene.

The most infamous phoney nature footage appeared in the 1958 Disney documentary *White Wilderness*. As part of its presentation of Arctic wildlife, the film showed lemmings jumping into a river to commit suicide, as legend has it they do. Except that lemmings don't really commit suicide: they sensibly avoid large bodies of water. To get the shot the filmmakers rounded up some lemmings and herded them off a cliff. As a result of this faked scene, lemming suicide became an accepted fact in popular culture for decades afterwards.

REALITY RULE 11.2

In real life no one has magical powers and stories don't always have happy endings.

Movies depend on the suspension of disbelief, but when the lights go up you're supposed to return to real life. This proves more difficult for some fans than for others.

Diehard fans of *Star Trek*, *Star Wars*, and *The Lord of the*

Rings are notorious for indulging the fantasy that the fictional worlds they love are real. You find them arguing over the finer points of the elvish language, or at conventions dressed as Spock or Princess Leia. Sometimes they even make real life correspond to their fantasies. *Star Wars* fans in Great Britain and Australia organized a campaign to list 'Jedi' as their religion on census forms. In both countries roughly as many Jedis as Jews were recorded. But *Star Trek* fans have all others beat. They organized a massive write-in campaign that succeeded in getting a space shuttle named after the fictional USS *Enterprise*. In a surreal twist, later *Star Trek* episodes showed a space shuttle mural in the captain's office, implying that the USS *Enterprise* was named for the Space Shuttle *Enterprise*. But the geek factor of even this achievement paled in comparison to the ongoing effort to make Klingon a real and thriving language.

Klingon came into existence as a speakable language thanks to Marc Okrand of the University of California, Berkeley. He created it in 1979 at the request of Paramount Pictures executives who wanted the Klingons in the first *Star Trek* movie to sound realistic. Okrand expanded the language for the third movie in the series and continues to add to it to this day. But it is the fans who have given the language an independent life.

A group of them banded together in 1992 to form the Klingon Language Institute, dedicated to the study and promotion of Klingon. Their efforts have been impressive. Two members, Andrew Strader and Nick Nicholas, translated Shakespeare's *Hamlet* into Klingon, inspired by General Chang's remark in *Star Trek VI: The Undiscovered Country* that 'Shakespeare is best read in the original Klingon'. Another member, Dr d'Armond Speers, attempted to raise his son as a

STAR TREK®

KLINGON HAMLET™

"taH pagh taHbe'!"
("To be or not to be!")

The Restored Klingon Version—
Prepared by the Klingon Language Institute

The Klingon Hamlet.

bilingual speaker of English and Klingon. From the day his son was born, Speers spoke only Klingon to him, while his wife spoke English. However, Speers had to abandon the experiment when his son stopped responding to Klingon. A major problem was that Klingon had no words for everyday items such as 'diaper' or 'table'.

Klingon received official recognition in 2003 when the Oregon mental health authority added the right to have a

Klingon interpreter to its list of patient privileges, noting, 'There are some cases where we've had mental health patients where this was all they would speak.' The decision was tongue-in-cheek (they've never really had a patient who speaks only Klingon), but should a Klingon wander off course, land on Earth, and find itself in an Oregon mental health facility, the officials there will be ready.

It's easy to tease science fiction and fantasy fans, but occasionally the blurring of movies and reality has more serious consequences. In 2001 a Japanese woman, Takako Konishi, was found frozen to death in the woods outside Fargo, North Dakota. Police who spoke to her a few days before her death believed she came to Fargo to search for a briefcase full of money that a character in the 1996 movie *Fargo* is shown burying in a snowy ditch. The officers had tried to explain to her that the movie is fiction (and, ironically, the movie's action does not take place in Fargo), but she didn't seem to understand, and off she went.

Video gamers can also lose the ability to distinguish between virtual and reality. In *Wired* magazine, Daniel Terdiman described one gamer who became so obsessed with the virtual challenge of picking up objects with a ball that, driving down Venice Boulevard (in real life), she found herself swerving to the side of the road to 'pick up' objects such as mailboxes. Other players have lost their jobs and families due to gaming addictions. Addicts can become so absorbed in their virtual worlds that they won't leave the computer to go to work, to say hello to a spouse, or even to use the bathroom – necessitating 'piss pots' beside the computer.

Sometimes the best thing you can do for yourself is turn off the TV, shut down the computer, take a walk around the block, and reacquaint yourself with the real world.

'In Hollywood it's good to be yourself, but it's even better to be someone else.'*

Modern society is full of people claiming to be celebrities they're not. At one end of this spectrum of imposters are those who do it for a living: celebrity lookalikes who entertain at corporate functions, fundraisers, and parties. Fake Elvis Presleys are so popular that they come in every shape, size, and form – fat, skinny, old, young, black, white, and airborne (as in the Flying Elvises featured in 1992's *Honeymoon in Vegas*). Buck Wolf, entertainment editor for ABCNEWS.com, has compiled a list of fake Elvii that includes Elvis Herselvis (the lesbian Elvis), Green E (the environmental Elvis who sings 'In the Landfill'), El Vez (the Mexican Elvis who sings 'In the Barrio'), Cop Elvis (a former New Zealand policeman fired for refusing to remove his blue suede shoes while on the job), and Extreme Elvis (a 350-pound stripteasing Elvis).

In many cases, celebrities pay others to impersonate them, in print. Literal-minded readers might assume an auto-biography is written by its subject. After all, the definition of an autobiography is 'an account of somebody's life written by that person'. But the more famous the person is, the more probable it is that they farmed out the menial task of writing to a lowly ghostwriter (who will be lucky if they get a thank you on the acknowledgements page).

This is understandable. Celebrities don't have time to write. But it's slightly more surprising when the 'author' of

---

* Geoff Pevere, 'Great fakery is the coin of the Hollywood realm', *Toronto Star*, 13 December 2002.

an autobiography doesn't read his own book. After Ronald Reagan's ghostwritten autobiography came out in 1990, the former president said, 'I hear it's a terrific book! One of these days I'm going to read it.' A joke, probably. But basketball player Charles Barkley sounded far more serious in 1993 when he read his own autobiography, after its publication, and publicly complained he had been 'misquoted' in it.

At the other end of the spectrum are con artists who pretend to be celebrities in order to perpetrate scams. The R&B singer Elgin Lumpkin should have had a double measure of immunity from such identity thieves. First there was his stage name: Ginuwine. Then there was the title of his hit song: 'Can You Tell It's Me'. Nevertheless, in 2001 a con artist walked away with $25,000 by posing as the singer and convincing concert promoters to send him deposits on future performances. One of his victims finally cottoned on to what was going on and warned him, 'We know you're not the real Ginuwine.' The faux Ginuwine is now serving time. Even more insidiously, there are so many little people who falsely claim to have played Oompa Loompas in 1971's *Willy Wonka and the Chocolate Factory* that this class of imposters has its own name: Oomposters.

Between the criminals and the professional lookalikes lurks a whole range of celebrity wannabes driven by a variety of motives – parody, wish-fulfilment, and ego-gratification among them. Weblogs, in particular, have become a vehicle for celebrity wannabes, due to the ease with which you can pretend to be anyone you want online. One of the more memorable fake celebrity blogs was the Bill Clinton journal that appeared in 2004 just as the former president launched a book tour to promote his autobiography. While Clinton's official memoirs may have been a bit dry, his (faux) weblog was far racier. The pseudo-Clinton divulged secrets such as his favourite sexual position (something he called 'the Terminator') and his nickname for Hillary ('the Dragon Lady').

Another popular faux blog claimed to be authored by Nick Nolte. It had the weathered actor musing on topics such as blenders, billiard tables, the 'blahs', and David Bowie's song 'Cat People'. (He wondered if Bowie was 'talking about cat people in the sense of some sort of society of cat mutations or if he just means humans who happen to like cats?') Nolte's blog attracted quite a following – including the real Nick Nolte's lawyer who sent its creators a cease-and-desist letter.

Many celebrities do maintain websites and weblogs, and will correspond with fans via email. But if you meet an A-list star in a random chat room, be sceptical. In 2004 a girl from Chile met a guy online who said he was Daniel Radcliffe, the actor who plays Harry Potter. She only realized he was lying after she travelled to England (with her mother), knocked on Daniel Radcliffe's door, and was told the actor had no idea who she was.

For some people impersonating their favourite celebrity online isn't enough. They want to become that celebrity in the flesh, and thanks to plastic surgery they can. In 2004 MTV debuted *I Want A Famous Face*, a programme that followed young people as they surgically refashioned themselves to look like their Hollywood idols. Episodes included a woman who turned herself into Kate Winslet, twins who turned into Brad Pitt, and (in what was probably the most notorious episode) a transsexual who transformed himself (herself?) into Jennifer Lopez.

While many people impersonate celebrities, a popular

conspiracy theory holds that certain celebrities are themselves imposters. This theory is most frequently applied to Paul McCartney, due to a persistent rumour that alleged the real Paul McCartney died in a car accident in 1966. Fans have scoured The Beatles' albums for clues that supposedly confirm the musician's death. For instance, play the *White Album* song 'Revolution 9' backwards and you might hear the phrase, 'Turn me on, dead man' – as clear a clue as any. So far Sir Paul has refused to admit he's a fake.

More recently a Scandinavian woman named Lisa Johansen claimed to be the real Lisa Marie Presley. According to her, for her own safety she was whisked away to Scandinavia shortly after the death of Elvis, and a body double was put in her place. She was to come out of hiding when she came of age, but the fake Lisa Marie usurped her position. Johansen claims that facial analysis proves her to be the real deal, but the other Lisa Marie doesn't seem to be losing any sleep over the challenge.

REALITY RULE 11.4

Technology can hide even the most glaring lack of talent.

Pop music is big business. Creating it requires teams of producers, sound engineers, and musicians – and an attractive face to sell it to the public. Whether the owner of that face can also sing is of secondary importance. Her voice can be improved or replaced entirely using technology. But for marketing reasons, the music industry likes to pretend otherwise. It pretends pop stars make their own music and can sing without a pant or a gasp while executing complex gymnastics routines during concerts. That this is simply not true has been proven by twenty years of lip-syncing scandals.

Milli Vanilli's 1988 singles 'Girl You Know It's True' and 'Blame It on the Rain' raced up the charts thanks in large part to the good looks and great dance moves of the group's singers, Rob and Fab. But after falling out with Rob and Fab, the group's producer, Frank Farian, disclosed in 1990 that the duo had sung neither on their debut album nor in concerts, but relied on anonymous studio vocalists. Rob and Fab's sole contribution was as eye candy for the crowds. The public backlash was swift and unforgiving. The duo were stripped of their Grammy award, and consumers filed a class-action suit against the group and their record company. Rob and Fab were banished to the twilight world of celebrity has-beens, and Milli Vanilli became the poster child of lip syncing.

The Milli Vanilli debacle scared the industry, but it didn't slow the lip-syncing phenomenon. Virtually all the major pop stars are rumoured to lip-sync during concerts. In October 2004 Ashlee Simpson became the latest star to be caught in a lip-syncing snafu. As she stood on a *Saturday Night Live* stage, her vocals began blaring through loudspeakers before she even had the microphone to her mouth. Her record company blamed this on a 'computer glitch', but Simpson's manager-father blamed his daughter's acid reflux. His convoluted logic was that she would normally never lip-sync, but her throat was sore, so she had to.

Singers aren't the only ones called upon to mime to pre-recorded music. Entire bands – it's rumoured virtually all the bands that appear on music shows – are reduced to stage furniture, mutely going through the motions of playing their instruments. From the point of view of concert promoters and the producers of live television shows, this insures against screw-ups – as long as the band doesn't rebel by stopping their act while the music continues.

Sometimes even the audience noise is faked. Television viewers have long been familiar with canned laughter, invented by engineer Charles Douglass in the 1950s. Laugh tracks' effectiveness (and thus their appeal to TV producers) lies in the fact that people tend to laugh when they hear other people laughing, and to cheer and clap when they hear others doing the same. Hearing silence makes people uncomfortable.

This psychological principle has not been lost on entertainment professionals outside the television industry. Engineers routinely dub in crowd noises on 'live' concert recordings to make the events sound more exciting. And, taking the concept a step further, stadium owners have been known to pipe in cheers and applause to loosen up audiences during sporting events. In 1997 the New York Mets management admitted to playing fake crowd noises over the speakers during home games at Continental Airlines Arena.

Soon real people won't be required at concerts at all. Taking the phenomenon to its logical end, pre-recorded band tracks can play in empty arenas to the cheers of fake crowds.

Reality Check

Question 1. The rock group Metallica sued the Canadian band Unfaith for using the chord progression E to F, claiming it had trademarked that sound. True or false?

Question 2. An American reality show challenged heterosexual men to compete to convince 'a jury of their queers' that they were gay. Challenges included pretending to come out to friends and going on blind dates with gay men. True or false?

Question 3. Channel 4 has announced plans to produce the ultimate reality show that will document the decomposition of the corpse of a volunteer. True or false?

Question 4. A reality show from 2004 locked contestants in a lab and exposed them to infectious diseases. The person who remained in the lab the longest won £100,000. True or false?

Question 5. A reality show produced in 2003 featured ten men stranded on an island with forty professional lap dancers. The winner was the man who resisted the temptations of the dancers longest. True or false?

ANSWERS

1. Metallica has been a vocal critic of file-sharing on the Internet. Therefore, when a press release appeared online in July 2003 claiming that Metallica was suing an obscure Canadian group to stop it from using the chord progression E to F, the story sounded plausible to many people. According to the press release, Metallica wanted to prevent Unfaith from causing 'confusion, deception and mistake in the minds of the public'. The release elaborated: 'We're not saying we own those two chords, individually – that would be ridiculous. We're just saying that in that specific order, people have grown to associate E, F with our music.' DJs railed against Metallica's action, and music fans denounced the band. However, the press release turned out to be a hoax concocted by Unfaith's lead singer, Erik Ashley. He had planted the story on his band's website, and backed it up

with a fake MTV news page. None of Unfaith's songs even used an E to F chord progression.

2. In May 2004 the Fox network announced that a reality programme based on the premise of heterosexual men having to successfully pretend they were gay would air in June. The show, as Fox's press release put it, would be a humorous take on 'a heterosexual male's worst nightmare'. It would be called *Seriously, Dude, I'm Gay*. The announcement was not a joke. The network had already filmed an episode. But after facing a huge backlash, Fox cancelled the series a few weeks later. *Seriously, Dude, I'm Gay* never aired.

3. True. In late 2004 Channel 4 did announce it was seeking a terminally ill patient willing to donate his or her corpse for such a show. A Channel 4 executive promised that the show would feature 'skin slipping off the body, the decaying; the maggot infestation and the bloating'. There is no word on when, or if, the show will air.

4. False. In early 2004 the *Daily Mirror* ran an ad seeking contestants for a reality show with this premise. The ad read: 'Could you be a guinea pig in our virology lab? Not worried about looking and feeling your worst on live TV? . . . Don't mind the nation seeing you at your lowest ebb? If you want to become a star in a week (and rich, too) then we want to hear from you.' Within a few days the paper had received over 200 applications. Medical doctors were horrified and blasted the concept in the press. However, the *Daily Mirror* later revealed the ad was an experiment 'to discover just how far people will go in their pursuit of fame'.

5. False. Channel 4 ran ads in mid-2003 encouraging men to apply to be on such a show, and soon it received over 20,000 applications. But in August the channel announced the concept was a hoax designed to promote *The Pilot Show*, a candid-camera-style comedy on which hoaxers fooled people into believing they were participating in absurd (but fake) reality programmes.

TWELVE

Advertising

The ancient Greeks confined all trade-related activities to marketplaces set off by clear boundaries. They believed that such dealings, though necessary, promoted antagonistic relationships. After all, sellers had a natural motive to lie and cheat, to say anything to get people to buy their products: *It's new and improved! It's got more stain-fighting power! It's now longer lasting!* The Greeks didn't want that dishonesty leaking into everyday life. Today we sporadically pay lip service to that ideal. For instance, we make a show of keeping advertising and news content separate in newspapers. But, in reality, the boundaries of our marketplaces have disappeared. Advertising is everywhere.

REALITY RULE 12.1
The most effective ads are the ones you're not aware of.

Say you've decided to buy a new digital camera. Which one should you purchase? You don't want to make a decision based solely on information from advertisers, so you go online to find reviews by actual users – the kind of reviews posted on message boards and sites such as Amazon.com. But don't assume all the reviews are genuine. In fact, marketeers write many of them. The practice is widespread. Hollywood studios routinely spam movie message boards with fake audience reviews of their latest releases. Authors use fake names to post glowing reviews of their own books (see Chapter Six). Even negative comments can't be trusted. They may be a marketeer's effort to discredit a rival company's product. The US Federal Trade Commission calls the practice 'disguised advertising'. It's illegal, but it happens anyway because it's so difficult to police.

Advertisers know that if a product endorsement appears to come from an independent source, it's far more credible than if it comes from them. So they go to great lengths to camouflage their advertising. The result is an ongoing effort to blur the line between advertising and all other forms of content – news, editorial, and entertainment.

Marketeers use techniques such as designing shopping catalogues to look like magazines (creating a hybrid entity known as a 'Magalog'). They pressure reporters to slip positive product mentions into articles. For instance, an article in a food magazine might list great restaurants in town, but not reveal that all the restaurants have paid to be mentioned. And they pay big money to get products placed prominently in movies, as well as in songs. In 2005 McDonald's offered rap artists who used the words 'Big Mac' in their lyrics up to $5 every time the track played on the radio.

The new great frontier for advertisers is the Internet, where the ultimate prize is to create an ad that 'goes viral'. Often this is done legitimately. That is, the advertisers don't hide the fact that the video clip or photograph is a commercial they created. But sometimes they do hide this information, in which case the ads are known as 'subvirals'. We've already seen one example of a subviral in Chapter Six – the video that seemed to show mobile phones popping popcorn, but was actually an ad designed to promote Bluetooth headsets.

A video clip popular in 2002 parodied the Mastercard 'priceless' ads. It started off as an innocent-looking scene of a young man saying goodnight to his date in front of her family's house but soon segued into something more risqué as he began to plead for oral sex. After some back and forth (she resists, he begs) the porch light suddenly came on, and the girl's sister opened the door to say, 'Dad says to go ahead and give him a blow job, or I can do it, or if need be he'll come down and do it himself, but for God's sake tell him to take his hand off the intercom.' A voiceover proclaimed: 'Having a girlfriend whose father has a sense of humour, priceless.'

The ad, which was viewed by millions of people, appeared to be a parody created by an amateur. However, the *Guardian* claimed to know from sources inside the advertising industry that it was actually 'produced in cahoots with Mastercard's US agency', thereby making it 'the highest-profile subviral yet'.

You don't need to turn on the Internet, or open a newspaper to be the victim of disguised advertising. It can happen to you if you just walk down the street or go to your neighbourhood bar. Marketeers hire actors to hang out undercover in bars and buy drinks for cool-looking people. The idea is to influence or 'lean on' trendsetters, in the hope that they'll adopt the product and get their friends to use it. Similarly, actors are hired to hang out in public and visibly use a product. Marketeers call this technique 'roach bait'. The consumers are the roaches, and the attractive actor is the bait.

Sony Ericsson Mobile Communications took this concept to a new level in 2002 when its marketing firm hired actors to prowl the streets of Manhattan posing as tourists. Their mission was to ask random pedestrians to take their picture using their new T68i digital camera/phone. Anyone who agreed would be given a rundown of the camera's snazzy features, without the actor ever breaking out of the chatty sightseer character. The campaign was dubbed Operation Fake Tourist. Female models were also hired to hang around in bars and strike up conversations in which they interwove references to their amazing new phone.

Conspiracy theorists will tell you that the phenomenon of disguised advertising goes even deeper – that for the past half-century advertisers have been hiding subliminal messages in movies and television shows. These messages supposedly send hypnotic commands straight to our subconscious brain, causing us to develop irresistible cravings for soda, popcorn, new cars, or cigarettes.

The concept of subliminal advertising entered popular culture in 1957 when ad-man James Vicary announced he had rigged a camera at a movie theatre in Fort Lee, New Jersey so that it flashed split-second messages such as, 'Hungry? Eat Popcorn' or, 'Drink Coca-Cola' during movies. The result, he claimed, was a sharp rise in concession sales.

The advertising industry instantly latched on to the idea. Radio stations began broadcasting sub-audible advertisements, only audible to the subconscious brain. A few even transmitted sub-audible public service announcements, secretly warning listeners to stay off icy roads. Vicary made a fortune by offering the consulting services of his Subliminal Projection Company.

The public, on the other hand, was terrified by the idea. However, tests repeatedly failed to find that subliminal ads had any measurable effect on consumer behaviour. So how had Vicary got his results? The answer came in 1962 when he admitted in an interview with *Advertising Age* that his Fort Lee experiment never happened. He had made it up.

In 1973 Wilson Bryan Key's book *Subliminal Seduction* reinvigorated the debate about subliminal advertising and added a new dimension to it. Key's titillating claim was that advertisers were embedding lurid sexual imagery in seemingly innocent ads. For instance, in a Sprite ad Key claimed he could see a hidden depiction of a woman having sex with a polar bear. In a later book he described spying an orgy in an ad for Howard Johnson's clam plate. These graphic sexual images apparently triggered consumers' carnal impulses, compelling them to buy the products.

Other rumoured subliminally seductive products include packs of Camel cigarettes that conceal a man with an erect penis in the front leg of the camel, and Pepsi cans that, stacked correctly, spell the word SEX. Pepsi withdrew these cans from the market in 1990 after it began receiving complaints.

Is there anything to the idea of subliminally seductive ads? It's likely that some artists hired to create ads do insert sexual imagery into them, just for the fun of it. It's also likely that some people see way more in advertising imagery than is really there. But just as with subliminal messages, there's no evidence such imagery (if it exists) has any influence on consumer behaviour. Anyway, advertisers don't need to resort to such tricks. Their other schemes and deceptions work so much better.

Advertisers are guilty of lying until proven innocent.

Advertisers are allowed to stretch the truth. They can make vague statements such as 'They're great!' or 'You'll love it!' Everyone knows the statements may not be literally true, but the law allows them to get away with it. The practice is called puffery.

But advertisers push the envelope as far as they can. You've probably received one of those letters that declare 'YOU'VE WON $10,000,000!' Maybe you tore it open, thinking it was for real, only to read the fine print inside: 'This is what we would be saying to you if you were our grand prize winner.' Technically the statement on the outside of the envelope is not a lie, so the advertiser can't be sued, but it's not honest either. It's a twisted truth. Other underhand schemes marketeers use to get people to open junk mail include designing letters to look like official documents, and making it look as though there's a cheque inside the envelope, though the cheque always turns out to be a phoney, uncashable promotional cheque.

In May 1995 Patrick Combs, a heavily in debt motivational speaker, received one of those promotional cheques made out for $95,093.35. It looked real – until he saw the word 'non-negotiable' stamped on it. But on a whim, he decided to deposit it at his bank's ATM machine to see what would happen. To his surprise, the bank credited the money to his account. Weeks later it was still there, so Combs had a teller write him out a cashier's cheque for the full amount. The next day the bank realized its mistake and asked for the money back, but Combs said no. In the United States banks are allowed a fixed period of time, usually about two weeks, in which they can identify bad cheques and deny funds. This period had expired, so legally the money was his.

Combs's scheme made headlines around the world. TV shows featured him, and Hollywood producers talked about turning his rags-to-riches story into a movie. Unfortunately, he ultimately had to return the money once it became clear the bank wasn't going to take no for an answer. However, he did turn his experience into a one-man show that earned him far more than $95,000, thus demonstrating what is perhaps the only way to make money from a promotional cheque.

The retail world is also full of twisted truths. Items are labelled 'Made in the USA' even if the only part made in the United States was a tag sewn on in Los Angeles or a bumper screwed on in North Carolina. Merchandise is marked at 'sale' prices, even if it was never sold at 'regular' price. (By law in the United States items must be offered at regular price 50 per cent of the time before a retailer can advertise them as reduced to sale price, but this regulation is widely ignored.) And then there's the ubiquitous practice of '99-centing', whereby retailers sell a product at $19.99 rather than $20, because they think consumers will believe it's cheaper.

Over the years, the editors of *Consumer Reports* have catalogued an enormous number of misleading claims made by retailers. Some of the all-time classics include the spoon advertised as a 'Microwave Spoon'. Consumers probably assumed this was a spoon that could be heated in the microwave. Not so! The fine print revealed it was 'not intended for use in microwave'. It was simply a spoon with which you could stir food that had been removed from a microwave – as you could with any other spoon.

Then there was the label on the outside of a VHS Storage Case that boasted the product 'automatically becomes portable when carried'. The Cleveland Finance Loan Company tempted loan seekers with the offer that they could 'pay nothing till first payment'. Dunkin' Donuts had a great deal for its customers: 'Free 3 muffins when you buy 3 at the regular 1/2 dozen price.' Finally, there was the car dealership that bragged of its half-price sale: 'The price you see is half the price you pay.' In other words, everything on the lot went for double the sticker price.

How companies display their products in ads also frequently stretches the truth. For instance, have you ever noticed how food in ads always looks better than it does in real life? The burgers look plump and sizzling in the commercials, but what you get at the store is a sad-looking patty. The phenomenon is called photoflattery, and it's the result of stylists who know how to make products look their best for the camera. In the food industry some of the tricks include shining fruit and vegetables with glycerin, using aspirin to give champagne extra fizz, and leaving hamburgers uncooked on the inside while searing them on the outside with a blowtorch to make them appear moister and plumper. Often the food you see in ads isn't food at all. Tobacco smoke stands in for steam. White glue is substituted for milk in cereal ads because the cereal won't go soggy in glue. And ice cream that doesn't melt is made out of Crisco and corn syrup.

McDonald's got in trouble for these practices in 2002. UK consumers complained that an ad for the restaurant's Steak Premiere sandwich showed a bun containing a substantial amount of steak, dressing, peppers and onions. However, the actual sandwich had far fewer ingredients. The Independent Television Commission investigated and concluded there was a 'disparity between the quantity of toppings against the television advertisements'. McDonald's admitted that, in making the ad, its photographers had moved the toppings to the edge of the bun to make them more visible. The ITC ordered the company to stop running the ad.

Advertisers usually get away with stretching the truth. However, the law prohibits them from making factually incorrect statements. If a company claims its product regrows hair and it doesn't, that's false advertising. Of course, just because it's illegal doesn't stop advertisers from doing it. Advertisers simply put the false claims in someone else's mouth. They create fake testimonials. For instance, the manufacturer of a penis-growth pill may shy away from making specific claims about the benefits of their product. Instead, they'll quote John from Muskogee who insists, 'I gained three inches in the first month.' John probably doesn't exist, but that's harder to prove.

It's not just fly-by-night companies that use the fake testimonial trick. Major corporations do it too. Apple Computer ran a high-profile 'switch campaign' in 2002 built around the premise of everyday computer users describing why they switched from Windows to a Mac. There's never been any suggestion that these testimonials were faked. But the success of Apple's campaign apparently got Microsoft jealous, because in 2002 it debuted its own 'switch' ad online. Beside a picture of a woman text read, 'After eight years as a Macintosh owner, I switched to a PC with Windows XP and Office XP. Why? It's about more and better . . .' Internet sleuths quickly deduced that the woman pictured was unlikely to have written the testimonial, because the photo came from a commercial library of stock images and had appeared in other ads. Ted Bridis, an Associated Press reporter, then discovered that the testimonial's author was Valerie Mallinson, a Microsoft PR rep. When challenged, Mallinson insisted the ad wasn't deceptive because she really had 'made the switch', but when the only switcher a company can drum up is its own PR rep, the endorsement isn't quite as persuasive. Microsoft quietly retracted the ad.

In an even more egregious example of fake testimonials, *Newsweek* revealed in 2001 that Sony Pictures had included quotations from a fictitious reviewer, David Manning, in print ads for many of its movies. Predictably, David Manning loved all the stinkers other reviewers panned, even praising the Rob Schneider comedy *The Animal* as 'another winner'. Sony pulled the ads, but defended the invented reviews as a form of free speech. When filmgoers filed a class-action suit, the judge ridiculed the free speech defence, and the company had to pay a $1.5 million settlement as well as $325,000 in fines to the state of Connecticut – making David Manning one of the most highly paid, or at least costly, movie reviewers in history.

An incident that occurred in the Czech Republic in 2003 cast a revealing light on the phenomenon of misleading ads. Flyers and billboards appeared around Prague promoting a new hypermarket, Cesky Sen (or 'Czech Dream'). The flyers promised it would be opening soon in the Letnany Fair-grounds, and that it would offer ultra-low prices such as TVs for £13 and mineral water for pennies, as well as a special surprise for anyone who came to the grand opening on 31 May. On the day of the opening, hundreds of consumers descended on the fairgrounds, shopping bags in hand, only to find nothing but a 26-by-260-foot Cesky Sen banner flut-tering in the wind. This was the special surprise.

In fact, there was no hypermarket, nor plans to build one. Student filmmakers Vit Klusak and Filip Remunda had set out to record what would happen when consumers' expecta-tions collided with reality. With the help of a grant from the

Czech Ministry of Culture they had hired an ad agency to launch a massive marketing blitz to promote a non-existent hypermarket.

As an angry, confused crowd grew in front of the Cesky Sen banner, Klusak and Remunda got on a stage to explain their project. Some people laughed; others booed and shouted curses at the filmmakers. A few kids threw rocks at the Cesky Sen sign. But the filmmakers were prepared for this and started playing music through speakers to calm the crowd. Eventually most people shrugged and went home.

Klusak and Remunda's point was that advertisers play with our expectations all the time, raising them with big promises only to let us down by delivering nothing. What Klusak and Remunda did was no different, except they put themselves on a stage where people could throw rocks at them.

REALITY RULE 12.3

All the world's an ad, and all the men and women potential billboards.

Advertisers don't see empty spaces. They only see branding opportunities. For instance, imagine hiking out in the mountains. You might see the snow-covered slopes surrounding you as an example of pristine beauty. Marketing executives see them as canvases waiting for an ad. At least, that's what occurred to the creative minds at SoCal Promotions who, in mid-2004, announced a plan to paint 'highly visible, unique, color advertisements' onto the snow of mountain ski slopes. Skiers, the company promised, wouldn't be able to avoid seeing them.

You can't even go to the bathroom without potentially

being bombarded by ads, thanks to Richard Deutsch, inventor of the Wizmark, the world's first 'interactive urinal communicator'. The device sits inside urinals and, when it senses motion, flashes lights and blares a taped message. There's also a version for women's toilets.

Marketeers seem to want to cover every surface in the world with an ad. This makes it difficult for anyone trying to satirize the advertising industry to outdo the weirdness of real life, because there seems to be no idea so bizarre that advertisers aren't willing to consider it. For instance, in 2000 Ted Fishman of *Esquire* magazine penned an April Fool's Day article about Freewheelz, a fictitious company that was supposedly going to give people free cars in return for the right to place advertisements inside and outside the car. Fishman thought the idea was obviously hare-brained, but upon publishing his spoof he discovered there were already companies, such as freecar.com, trying that exact business model.

Likewise, when Rolling Rock beer launched a hoax campaign in 2008 in which they claimed they were going to beam ads onto the surface of the moon, they were merely echoing an idea that other marketing executives had already considered. In 1999 Coca-Cola had seriously explored the concept of 'moonvertising'. Their executives determined it was technologically possible to use lasers to beam the image of a Coke logo onto the moon, but they had to abandon the idea because the Federal Aviation Administration forbade it, fearing the lasers might interfere with aircraft.

Those listening to the 1 April 1994 edition of National Public Radio's *All Things Considered* heard that companies such as Pepsi had begun to sponsor corporate logo tattoos. In return for permanently branding themselves, teenagers would receive a lifetime 10 per cent discount on that company's

Andrew Fischer, the human billboard, in Times Square.

products. Teenagers were said to be responding enthusiastically. The news was an April Fool's Day spoof. NPR thought that people walking around with ad tattoos was too ridiculous to ever happen. But again, they were wrong. In 2003 Justin Kapust, a student at Johnson & Wales University in Rhode Island, launched Headvertise, a company that paid college students $70 a week to wear temporary tattoos on their foreheads. Soon after, the ad firm Night Agency debuted 'ass-vertising'. This involved 'putting a logo, a web address, or a brief message on the seat of a pair of bikini-style panties. The panties are then worn by beautiful girls, and revealed when appropriate in a "mooning" fashion.'

However, body ads really attracted the attention of the mainstream media in January 2005, when twenty-year-old Andrew Fischer of Omaha, Nebraska auctioned on eBay one month's advertising space on his forehead. It's not clear why Andrew's offer received so much more publicity than earlier body ad schemes – maybe he had a bigger forehead – but whatever the case, the winning bidder gave him $37,375 to advertise its snoring remedy and whisked him away on a month-long publicity tour that included appearances on *Good Morning America* and *Inside Edition*.

Inspired by Andrew's success, would-be body advertisers tendered space on every available body part: forehead, cleavage, buttocks, as well as, in one case, a pregnant belly. One extreme capitalist was even willing to let advertisers tattoo their logo inside his body, on his colon.

The lesson is, never put anything past the advertising industry – no matter how tasteless, ridiculous, or absurd the idea may sound. In fact, the more outrageous a concept is, the more likely it is that it will appeal to a marketeer.

Reality Check

Question 1. A penis can be seen in the cover art for Disney's *The Little Mermaid*. True or false?

Question 2. An Australian ad agency trained flocks of geese to fly in formation and skywrite (or 'birdtype') letters and corporate logos. True or false?

Question 3. A Denver-based agency attempted to place advertisements on beggars' 'will work for food' signs. True or false?

Question 4. A videogame company promoted one of its games by installing advertisements at UK bus stops that featured fake blood oozing out of cartridges, seeping down the inside of a clear plastic sheet, and dripping onto the street. Cleaners were hired to periodically wash the 'blood' off the pavement. True or false?

Question 5. An ad for Puma sneakers that ran in the Brazilian version of *Maxim* showed a young woman kneeling suggestively in front of a man visible from the thighs down. Some kind of milky liquid had landed on the woman's thigh. True or false?

Question 6. A 2005 ad for the Volkswagen Polo showed a suicide bomber detonating himself inside a Polo outside a street-front café. However, the car contained the explosion without suffering any damage. The slogan 'Polo. Small but tough' then appeared on-screen. True or false?

ANSWERS

1. Those who believe that advertisers routinely use 'subliminal seduction' to promote their products often single out the Disney Corporation as being one of the worst offenders when it comes to hiding erotic material in seemingly innocent images. And in the case of *The Little Mermaid*, it is true that the original cover art for the video of this movie included a castle tower that was obviously phallus-shaped. This appeared to be a case of an artist's joke, rather than a purposeful attempt by Disney to subliminally seduce consumers. The artist swore he didn't notice the phallic tower until it was pointed out to him later, though the shape of the tower is so obvious that this denial barely seemed credible. The hidden body part caused such an uproar once Christian groups cottoned on to it that Disney removed it from the later laser disc release of the movie.

Other infamous examples of supposed Disney erotica include: an erection that the minister at Ariel's wedding in *The Little Mermaid* seems to sport (Disney explains the bulge away as his knee); the word SEX that forms in a cloud of dust halfway through *The Lion King* when Simba lies down on a cliff (Disney admits something is there, but says the letters spell SFX, a reference to the special effects team that worked on the movie); the phrase 'All good teenagers take off your clothes' that the title character in *Aladdin* is said to whisper while standing on a palace balcony with Princess Jasmine (Disney claims he's saying, 'Scat, good tiger, take off and go'); and an image of a nude woman that appeared in a single frame of *The Rescuers*. The reality of *The Rescuers* nudity was confirmed when Disney recalled 3.4 million copies of the video in 1999 after realizing that a prankster had indeed inserted the offending frame.

2. Australian writer Stephen Banham described skywriting geese in *Fancy*, a book that mixed factual and fictional stories about typography. Birdtyping was one of the fictional concepts. Advertisers have never attempted this, mainly because it is beyond their abilities. In Banham's story, the bird trainer was starting his flock with a simple logo: V for Volvo. Curved letters, he noted, were going to take the birds a bit longer to learn.

3. In May 2002 Denver-based Sumaato Advertising did attempt to convince panhandlers to hold 'will work for food' signs that were branded with corporate logos. Employees of the ad agency drove around the city handing out these new signs to the homeless. No money was exchanged. The panhandlers simply got more attractive signs in return for giving the ad agency free publicity. Critics blasted Sumaato for trivializing the homeless problem. The agency claimed it only meant to raise awareness of the issue. Nevertheless, the

idea did not prove viable. There were too few sponsors willing to use the homeless as mobile billboards.

4. True. Acclaim Entertainment promoted the ultra-gory game *Gladiator: Sword of Vengeance* with a 'bloodvertising' campaign that ran for a week.

5. False. An image purporting to be a Puma 'oral sex' ad circulated widely online in early 2003, but it never appeared in any version of *Maxim*, and Puma strongly denied any connection to it. The company even threatened legal action against anyone who reproduced it. Even after this denial many bloggers continued to speculate that Puma might have created the ad in order to generate online buzz, but there is no evidence to support this theory. Other theories that circulated online (all unsupported by any evidence) were that Puma's rival Adidas created the image; that it was a spec ad (speculative ad-agencies create these to show potential clients the work they're capable of); that it was an in-house joke produced by someone at Puma but never intended for public viewing; or that it was the work of an unknown photoshop-skilled prankster. No one has stepped forward to take credit for the racy Puma ad, so the image remains an unsolved mystery.

6. False. This ad circulated widely online in early 2005 and generated enormous controversy, but Volkswagen denied any involvement in its creation. It was eventually revealed to be a spec ad made by professional filmmakers LAD (Lee and Dan). Reportedly Lee and Dan spent £40,000 to make the ad, since they shot it on 35mm film, but due to the controversy, they probably didn't get any of Volkswagen's business. According to rumour, the Royal Society for the Prevention of Accidents complained that the suicide bomber wasn't wearing a seat belt.

THIRTEEN

Business

P. T. Barnum, the nineteenth-century master of the hoax, wrote in his book *The Humbugs of the World*, 'It would be a wonderful thing for mankind if some philosophic Yankee would contrive some kind of "ometer" that would measure the infusion of humbug in anything. A "Humbugometer" he might call it.' This machine, Barnum mused, would sniff out all kinds of humbugs – such as watered-down milk or snake-oil medicine – fobbed off by businessmen upon the public. Such a device would still be very useful today. After all, humbug (or bullshit as we now call it) seems to be the lifeblood of modern business.

REALITY RULE 13.1

Money is real only if everyone agrees to pretend it's real.

Money has no inherent value. It's just paper (or metal) unless people are willing to accept that it represents something more. Its value is an illusion that everyone plays along with because it's more convenient to carry paper in your wallet than to cart around things of real value, such as cows or sheep.

But while paper money is more convenient than bartered goods, it's also a lot easier to fake. And lots of people do fake it. Federal authorities in the US estimate that over $40 million worth of counterfeit money is spent every year, and the amount is growing rapidly because of the ease with which colour copiers and printers can be used for counterfeiting. If you find yourself stuck with counterfeit money, you're supposed to report it to the police. But don't expect a refund. The only way to recover your loss is to trick someone else into taking the stuff. But that, of course, would be illegal.

Most counterfeiters go to great lengths to make their fake currency look convincing – at least under casual scrutiny – but some don't bother. These are the slacker counterfeiters. They rely entirely on the gullibility of their victims, which often is a fairly good strategy. For instance, on 28 January 2001 a man drove up to a drive-through window at a Dairy Queen in Danville, Kentucky and paid for his $2.12 purchase with a $200 George Bush bill. The front of the bill showed a likeness of George Bush and a treasury seal marked, 'The right to bear arms'. The back showed an oil well and the White House lawn decorated with signs such as, 'No more scandals' and, 'We like broccoli'. The cashier happily accepted the bill and gave $197.88 in change – at which point the customer quickly drove off. The cashier later explained that she had believed the $200 bill to be legitimate because it was green, just like real money.

European cashiers have proven no better than Americans at spotting obvious fakes, especially during the confusion that surrounded the switch to euros as Europe's official

Non-negotiable currency.

currency. In January 2002 a bartender in southern France accepted Monopoly money from a customer, having mistaken it for the new currency. Soon afterwards German authorities discovered shoppers were using fake 300 and 1000-euro notes adorned with pictures of buxom naked women. The European central bank had given the firm Planet-Present permission to distribute the bills as a publicity stunt, never realizing people might think the erotic money was real.

For every cashier who accepts obviously fake money, there's a counterfeiter who pushes her luck too far. Take Alice Regina Pike, who, in an apparent bid for the title Stupidest Criminal Ever, asked a Wal-Mart cashier to cash a $1,000,000 bill. When the cashier refused, Pike tried to use the bill to buy $1,675 worth of merchandise. Still no luck. Finally the store called the cops who took Pike away.

Then there were the hapless counterfeiters who successfully used their phoney bills to buy $300 worth of merchandise at Wal-Mart, but came back to the store a few days later to return the merchandise for real money. The cashier recognized the merchandise and handed back the bogus bills. The thieves walked out of the store, did a U-turn, and returned to complain that the money was counterfeit. The store manager told them if they had a problem with that, they could go to the police. They were never seen again.

Stores try to be vigilant, but sometimes their caution goes too far, and they end up refusing legitimate bills, believing them to be counterfeit. When this happens, the most frequent culprits are counterfeit-detection pens. These widely used pens contain a solution that reacts with starch to produce a black line. The expensive fibre used to make real currency doesn't contain starch, whereas the cheap paper commonly used to make counterfeit money does. So a black line should only appear on the fake stuff, unless starch got onto real money, which can happen for any number of reasons. For instance, if a person decides to iron their bills with starch (neat freaks are known to do this), this will cause them to be flagged incorrectly as fake.

Finally, not everyone who creates fake money is a counterfeiter. There are a number of artists who use their skills to produce fake money because they find inspiration in the tension between money's aesthetic and economic functions. Stephen Barnwell has created currency for the fictional land of Nadiria, as well as a history that explains how this lost colony of Antarctica was founded in 1866 and survived for thirty-three years until it mysteriously vanished. Nadiria's history can be read, and samples of its 'Dream-Dollars' bought, at dream-dollars.com.

J. S. G. Boggs's fascination with money has led him much closer to the edge of the law. His drawings of dollars, euros, or whatever the currency is where he happens to be, are realistic enough to be mistaken for actual money, except that he leaves one side blank (save for his signature and thumb-print). He 'spends' his work in stores or restaurants by finding people willing to accept it at the face value it depicts, in exchange for goods or services. It's smart to take Boggs's offer, because collectors track down these 'Boggs bills' and buy them for well upward of ten times their face value.

However, his art hasn't made Boggs many friends at treasury departments around the world. He's been charged with counterfeiting in Britain and Australia (in both cases juries found him not guilty), and the American Secret Service raided his studio in 1992 and confiscated thousands of his works. The Secret Service refuses to return these works, although it has never charged Boggs with a crime.

Ironically, as Boggs's fame has grown, counterfeit Boggs bills – fakes of fakes – have started popping up. However, this doesn't concern Boggs. He told one collector who bought a Boggs bill for $2,000, only to learn it was the work of a copycat, not to worry. He figured the fake was a good one, so she got her money's worth.

REALITY RULE 13.2

The most important skill in any office is the art of B.S.

It's called the Shirk Ethic. It's the belief that you should never put in an honest day's work if you can fake it instead. Thus ensues an elaborate cat-and-mouse game between employees and bosses – a game that almost every worker participates in, to one degree or another.

The most common office scam, by far, is the fake sickie. Americans call it 'taking a mental health day'. In both Britain and America one-third of polled workers admit to having taken fake sick days, though the real number is probably much higher. According to surveys, British doctors suspect over 40 per cent of requests they receive for sick notes are bogus. Career Builder, an online employment agency, has collected examples of unusual sick-day excuses that include: 'I tripped over my dog and was knocked unconscious,' 'I was sprayed by a venomous snake,' and 'A hitman was looking for me.'

A related phenomenon – telling co-workers that you're going on vacation while you actually stay at home – happens more often than one might think. In Italy, where taking expensive vacations gives important bragging rights at the office, a 2003 poll conducted by the psychologists' association Help Me found that almost 7 per cent of respondents planned to lie about where they went. People go so far as to tell their neighbours they're leaving. Then they buy a sunlamp, sit at home soaking up the rays, and resurface a week later with a great tan. Back at the office they regale co-workers with tales of the Riviera resort where they stayed.

The second most common office scam is padding the CV, known euphemistically as 'putting your best foot forward', or 'jazzing up your qualifications'. In a 2002 survey commissioned by Office Angels, a UK temp agency, 80 per cent of respondents admitted they were willing to fudge their CV. The other 20 per cent, presumably, were lying. Common forms of CV padding include altering the dates of previous employment (to cover embarrassing gaps) and exaggerating former job titles, duties, and salaries. But the most serious lies concern education.

In today's workplace having an advanced degree can translate into higher pay, and having attended a prestigious university such as Stanford, Harvard, or Oxford can be an important status symbol. So job-seekers have a lot of incentive to invent degrees, and not much to deter them from doing so. For instance, lying about a degree is illegal in only a handful of American states, and even then it's a misdemeanour, warranting a small fine but no jail time.

During the 1980s, in a rare example of a crackdown on CV padders, the FBI busted approximately 12,000 people, working in a variety of professions. They called it Operation Dipscam, short for Diploma Scam. More recently a string of high-profile executives have been caught with phoney diplomas listed on their CVs, including the ex-CFO of Veritas Software, Kenneth Lonchar (fake degree from Stanford Business School) and the ex-CEO of Bausch & Lomb, Ronald Zarella (unearned MBA from New York University). Ironically, lying about education is most popular in the field of education itself, since teachers' salaries are often tied directly to their academic credentials.

For those who don't want to invent a fake degree out of thin air, a vast market of diploma mills stand ready and willing to help. These are fly-by-night 'colleges' and 'universities' that grant degrees to anyone for the right price. A typical example is Glencullen University, which sounds like it might be a legitimate Irish university, but is actually based in Romania and has no campus and no faculty. A similar institution is Saint Regis, which in 2004 eleven teachers in Georgia were found to have advanced degrees from. It's a Liberian college that asks very little of its students (nothing but payment, actually).

Recently there have been reports of a new variety of office scam. Employees are said to be outsourcing their own jobs, and pocketing the difference. The *Times of India* has claimed this to be an especially popular trend among programmers.

They cited an example of a programmer who received a $67,000 contract for a job and outsourced it to a developer in India whom he paid $12,000. The programmer, who told his boss he was telecommuting, only had to spend ninety minutes a day supervising the code.

To many such a practice might sound like theft, but its defenders argue that the employee who outsources his own labour is merely profiting from the surplus value of another's work. And, after all, isn't this how all companies make their profits? No less an authority than Karl Marx stated that it is the principle upon which capitalism is founded. But if you are outsourcing your own job, don't try making this argument to your employer. You're likely to be shown the door, and the Indian programmer hired in your place.

REALITY RULE 13.3

Nothing separates a person from his sanity like the promise of easy money.

Give a person the idea there's a quick and easy way to make a lot of money, and their grip on reality rapidly comes undone. This is evidenced by the speculative bubbles that have been a recurring theme throughout the history of finance. They feature people, en masse, throwing money at dumb investments simply because everyone else is doing the same.

The first (and arguably most famous) bubble of the modern era was the seventeenth-century tulip craze in Holland. In 1636 word spread that wealthy people were willing to pay fantastically large sums of money for tulips, especially rare 'mosaic' varieties that displayed brilliant flames of colour. Prices were soon bid up, with a large portion of the population joining in the speculative fervour. People traded their life savings for bulbs, believing they could resell them at windfall profits. At the height of the mania a single rare bulb could fetch as much as a mansion. Charles Mackay, author of *Extraordinary Popular Delusions and the Madness of Crowds*, records that one unfortunate sailor arrived in Holland during the excitement and ate a tulip bulb he found on a merchant's counter because he mistook it for an onion; for this heinous crime, he spent months in jail. But the mania was short-lived. By 1637 panic selling commenced as people realized they were never going to make a return on their investments. The price of bulbs crashed, and many people were ruined.

Eighty years after the tulip mania, the belief that there was huge money to be made from trade with the Americas triggered speculative bubbles in France and England. There actually was huge money to be made, but nowhere near as fast or as effortlessly as speculators hoped.

The Scottish financier John Law led the mania in France. As head of the Mississippi Company he talked up the seemingly limitless profits his venture stood to make from its monopoly on trade with the Mississippi region. The company's stock began to rise, and early investors made spectacular profits, leading to even greater excitement. The value of the company swelled dramatically until the summer of 1720, then collapsed. Share prices declined by 97 per cent, the company went bankrupt, and the economy of France was put in jeopardy. Law had to flee the country and died penniless in 1729.

In England a similar debacle unfolded as investors bid up shares of the South Sea Company, which boasted monopoly rights on trade with the South Seas. Schemers took advantage of the nation's speculative mood by offering all kinds of hare-brained investment opportunities, almost all of which found eager subscribers. These small-scale schemes were dubbed 'bubbles', eventually giving name to the larger phenomenon. One bubble proposed to revolutionize the art of war by designing square cannon balls. Another invited the public to invest – with returns of over 100 per cent every year – in 'A company for carrying on an undertaking of great advantage, but nobody to know what it is.' Within a day people had snatched up almost 1,000 shares – whereupon the scheme's inventor took the money and ran, never to be seen again.

The South Sea house of cards came tumbling down in late 1720 when the company's value crashed. Complete financial disaster was averted thanks to actions of the British government, but huge numbers of people lost everything. Surprisingly, the South Sea Company survived the crisis and endured, in a reorganized form, until the 1850s.

In the coming years, popular excitement about new forms of transportation spawned a series of bubbles – in canal stocks during the 1830s, railroad stocks during the 1870s, and automobile and airline stocks during the roaring 1920s. Demand for airline stocks became so great after Charles Lindbergh's 1927 transatlantic flight that any stock with the word 'airline' in its name posted massive gains – including, notoriously, Seaboard Air Lines, a railway company. The bubbles of the 1920s ended with the Great Depression of the 1930s.

By the early 1960s bitter memories of the Great Depression were fading, and investors were looking for the next big thing. They found it in electronics. Any company with a variation of the term 'tronics' in its name became a stock market darling, propelling firms such as Circuitronics and Videotronics to dizzying heights and earning the bubble the nickname the Tronics Boom. The boom crashed in 1962.

But investors' passion for technology hadn't abated. It surged again in the 1980s with the biotech bubble, and reached a crescendo during the dot-com mania of the 1990s. In theory dot-com investors were excited about the communications revolution the Internet was facilitating. But in practice this excitement translated into a blind rush to buy the stock of any company with '.com' in its name. Purdue University professor Panambur Raghavendra Rau calculated that during the height of the mania a company could add 28 per cent to the value of its stock *in a single day* simply by adding .com to its name, even if the company had nothing to do with the Internet. He cited the example of Go-Rachels.com, which profited from its .com suffix despite being a potato-chip maker lacking any connection to the Internet. The business didn't even have a website.

Dot-com-enamoured speculators gave companies that were little more than web portals valuations of billions of dollars. It didn't matter if the companies were making no money and couldn't explain how they planned to make money. Legend tells of a company that lured investors with a vague mission statement promising to 'develop cool stuff', thereby offering the 1990s' equivalent of 'an undertaking of great advantage, but nobody to know what it is'.

The dot-com bubble deflated slowly but relentlessly throughout 2000, leaving hundreds of thousands of portfolios in tatters. In the temporary backlash that followed, any association with the Internet became anathema. Rau estimated that during this period companies could add an average of 29 per cent to their value by dropping '.com' from their names.

Investors lost money but not their enthusiasm. The dot-com bubble proved to be a mere warm-up for the Great Real

Estate Bubble that popped in 2008. Hundreds of thousands of people with questionable credit had been buying homes, often with little or no money down. As interest rates adjusted, and these people discovered they could no longer afford their loans, banks started to go under, triggering a global financial meltdown said to be the worst since the Great Depression of the 1930s. Telling the investors and homeowners who have lost everything that such financial ups and downs are nothing new is cold comfort indeed.

REALITY RULE 13.4
A good accountant knows that two plus two equals four. A great accountant knows that two plus two equals whatever you want it to equal.

When a company employs thousands of people and generates billions of dollars in revenue, its size alone seems to offer a guarantee of legitimacy. But such appearances can be deceptive. The history of business is full of massive companies that were exposed as nothing more than megascams.

At the start of the twentieth century, Swedish businessman Ivan Kreuger controlled 40 per cent of world match production and stood at the helm of a massive financial empire. He had assets worth (in modern money) over $100 billion, and by the 1920s his companies' stocks and bonds were the most widely held in the world. But the market crash of 1929 put a serious dent in his finances and sent his business into a tailspin. He committed suicide in 1932 (or faked it, according to persistent rumours), after which auditors realized his empire was nothing but a gigantic pyramid scheme. He had orchestrated a bewildering array of subsidiary companies, four hundred in total, which artificially propped one another up by extending each other credit. His total debt exceeded that of the country of Sweden.

Anthony 'Tino' De Angelis was head of the Allied Crude Vegetable Oil Refining Corporation. At the peak of his operation, in the early 1960s, he claimed to have almost two billion pounds of vegetable oil sitting in his New Jersey storage tanks. Never mind that his tanks could hold, at most, sixty million pounds, or that two billion pounds was more than the entire annual world production. On the basis of having all this oil he was able to borrow billions of dollars (inflation adjusted).

The American Express Field Warehousing Corporation was supposed to verify that De Angelis had all the oil he claimed, and it occasionally sent someone to look at his tanks. Everything seemed to be in order, so the money kept flowing. But with this money De Angelis was buying futures in oil, betting its price would go up. Instead the price went down, and De Angelis found himself unable to repay his loans. When his creditors came to take possession of his collateral, they discovered there was hardly any oil.

De Angelis's secret was that underground pipes connected the tanks. When an inspector came, he would see a full tank. But as he moved along the line, that tank would quickly be emptied and the oil piped to the next tank the inspector wanted to see. In 1965 De Angelis was sentenced to twenty years in prison (of which he served seven). It's estimated that almost $4 billion disappeared into his empty oil tanks.

In 1985 Ken Lay became CEO of a company named InterNorth, renamed it Enron, and launched it on a path towards global domination of the power industry. Over the next fifteen years the company grew at a staggering rate, and investors fell in love with it, despite rumours about its unsavoury business practices. For instance, it was widely alleged that by convincing power plants to shut down for unneeded repairs Enron engineered a phoney energy crisis that slammed Californians with record-high energy prices in 2000. Nevertheless, by 2001 Enron was America's seventh-largest corporation – on paper. But a mounting pile of debt and losses lurked behind the company's profitable veneer.

Part of Enron's success strategy was pure showmanship. Employees later confessed they were occasionally required to man a phoney trading floor on the sixth floor of the corporate headquarters. To convince visiting Wall Street analysts of how productive and energetic the firm was, they would pretend to be busy making deals. Employee Carol Elkin described the trading floor to the *Wall Street Journal* as 'an elaborate Hollywood production'.

More significantly, Enron used accounting magic to create the illusion of enormous profitability. It hid debt in 'special purpose vehicles' – phoney subsidiary companies designed for this purpose. It also claimed decades' worth of predicted future profit as present-day profit. This would be like claiming on a loan application that you make a salary of $300,000 because you expect to earn $30,000 a year for the next ten years. The company's supposed riches drove up the stock price, and company executives profited from the ballooning price by giving themselves generous stock options.

Enron executives kept up the pretence of profitability until the very end. In August 2001 Ken Lay sent his employees an email that read, 'I have never felt better about the prospects for the company.' Three months later the company filed for bankruptcy, revealing it was over $16 billion in debt. It was the largest corporate bankruptcy in US history.

Finally, we have Bernard Madoff, head of Bernard L. Madoff Investment Securities LLC, which he founded in 1960. This was one of the most prestigious firms on Wall Street. It acted both as a market-maker (a middleman between buyers and sellers of shares) and as an investment fund that managed money for high-net-worth individuals and institutions. Year after year Madoff delivered reliable annual returns of around 10 per cent for his investors. He managed to do this even in down markets when everyone else was losing money. A few people did openly question how he pulled this off, but billions of dollars continued to be entrusted to him, because he always paid out if anyone requested their money.

The end came swiftly for Madoff. The FBI arrested him in December 2008 and charged him with securities fraud. It now appears he was operating one of the largest pyramid schemes in history. He had been paying some investors (those who requested their money) with money from other investors. The scheme went belly-up when clients wanted to withdraw over $7 billion from the firm due to the ongoing economic crisis. Madoff simply didn't have this money. Losses are estimated to be as high as $50 billion.

These megascams affirm the old truism that if you're going to lie, lie big. Suckers are always more willing to believe a big lie rather than a little one.

Reality Check

Question 1. McDonald's has experimented with outsourcing the job of taking orders at its drive-through windows to long-distance call centres. True or false?

Question 2. Some players of online multi-user games such as *Final Fantasy* outsource the tedious parts of games to workers in poor countries. True or false?

Question 3. The BBC has installed 'mutter machines' in some of its offices. These machines emit background noises of conversation and laughter to make workers feel as if they're working in an upbeat environment. True or false?

Question 4. The miniskirt index, which tracks the number of miniskirts purchased, is one of many economic indicators that economists use to gauge the strength of the economy. True or false?

ANSWERS

1. McDonald's *has* experimented with outsourcing the drive-through window ordering process such that, at a drive-through in Oregon, a customer could give their order to someone in North Dakota, who then transmits it back to the restaurant in Oregon. According to rumour, this was an attempt to cut costs by outsourcing the jobs to states with a lower minimum wage, but McDonald's denies this. It insists the experiment was all about increasing efficiency – as employees who have to take orders over the drive-through microphone and deliver food at the same time often make mistakes.

2. Gamers are notorious for finding ways to hack the system, whether it's cheating with secret codes or, yes, paying people to play the boring parts for them. As reported in *Wired* magazine, in countries such as Russia and China workers are paid to play online games for one purpose – to earn in-game

goods and currency that can then be sold to outfits, such as Internet Gaming Entertainment (IGE), that resell them to Westerners.

3. The accountants who worked at the BBC's finance department in west London complained that their offices were too quiet. This is a fairly common complaint in modern workspaces. It's known as 'pin-drop syndrome'. The combination of double-glazed windows, carpeting, and efficient air-conditioning can make offices almost noiseless, and workers say the effect is unnerving. To counter this problem, in 1999 the BBC developed a 'mutter machine' that played background chatter simulating the sound of people working. However, when the BBC announced what it had done, the media ridiculed the idea, and so the BBC stopped providing any further information about it.

4. True. The Consumer Price Index (CPI), which tracks the prices of common household goods in order to reveal inflationary trends, is the best known economic indicator used by economists. However, many other indices exist, and some of them, such as the miniskirt index, are somewhat fanciful. The miniskirt index is particularly popular in Japan. Increased miniskirt sales are said to indicate the economy is doing, or will do, well. The argument is that the purchase of the miniskirt not only indicates optimism and vanity, emotions expressed more strongly in good times, but also has an economic effect of its own. First, it helps the clothing industry; second, miniskirts are usually worn when going out to show off, and more people going out benefits the food, beauty, and entertainment industries; and third, miniskirts stimulate men, leading them to increase their economic activity as they strive to impress miniskirt-wearers.

Another unusual economic indicator is the Cocktail Party Chatter Index (CPCI), which correlates the amount of cocktail party chatter about a stock or commodity to its future value. A lot of talk about a stock is a bearish indicator that means its value will go down. (Once everybody knows about a stock it's been overbought and can only head south.)

FOURTEEN

Politics

Modern politicians, if they want long careers, must embrace several core assumptions. The first is that what they've done isn't as important as what people *think* they've done. The second is that being honest isn't as important as *looking* honest. They disregard these principles at their peril. They can be sure their opponents aren't disregarding them.

REALITY RULE 14.1

Politics is the art of looking good on TV.

Stagecraft has always been an essential part of politics. According to legend, when Catherine the Great toured Crimea in 1787, Russian field marshal Grigori Aleksandrovich Potemkin built fake villages along her route in order to hide the poverty of the region from her. The modern-day political equivalent of these Potemkin villages is the Potemkin crowd. As politicians tour the country during their campaigns, the last thing their handlers want is for them to show up in a town and have no one attend their rally. Or, even worse, to have a hostile crowd show up. It looks very bad on TV. The solution is ready-made crowds. Docile, friendly supporters are bussed in so that the politician always appears on camera speaking to a large, enthusiastic audience.

For instance, in March 2004 President Bush made a campaign stop in Bay Shore, New York where he delivered a lunchtime speech to a cheering audience. Bush smiled for the cameras, shook a few hands, and then moved on. But a reporter who lingered on afterwards discovered that many of the people in the crowd didn't speak English and had no idea what the president had said. They were workers from a local auto parts factory who had been brought in on their lunch break to fill up the room. They had been instructed to wave and cheer.

Sometimes politicians still tour fake villages. During Queen Elizabeth's 2003 state visit to Nigeria, she was photographed touring a village market and chatting with local people. Except Nigerian security officials felt it would be too dangerous for the Queen to go out in public, so instead the Queen walked through a fake village, manned by actors, on the set of a soap opera, inside an armed compound. The real Nigerian villagers had to try to get a glimpse of her through the compound's perimeter wall.

In political lore, the event that has come to symbolize the importance of media imagery, particularly TV images, is the Nixon–Kennedy debate of 1960. This was the first American presidential debate to be broadcast on TV. However, Nixon was recovering from the flu and looked pale and unshaven. Also, he didn't use make-up. Kennedy, by contrast, looked tanned, relaxed, and energetic, and he did use make-up. Historians agree that this was a crucial factor in helping Kennedy win the election. Taking this lesson to heart, political handlers have ever since been keenly aware of how their candidate looks on TV. Which is why a politician's make-up artist has become as important a part of their staff as their speechwriter.

However, sometimes the make-up artists go a little overboard. The day before the first of the 2004 US presidential debates, John Kerry showed up in public looking oddly pumpkin-coloured. Apparently his handlers had liberally slathered him with tanning lotion in anticipation of the debate, mistakenly turning him orange. Kerry lost the election.

Although political handlers go to great lengths to control the images that the public sees, there are limits to what they can do. They are ultimately constrained by reality. The most notorious example of this in recent years occurred on 1 May 2003 when President Bush co-piloted a Navy jet that touched down on the USS *Abraham Lincoln*, where he met soldiers returning from the war in Iraq. Standing on the deck of the carrier, Bush announced the end of major combat operations in Iraq as a 'Mission Accomplished' banner rippled in the breeze behind him. The moment, which had been entirely scripted by Bush's handlers, was supposed to showcase a heroic, successful president who had once been a fighter pilot in the Texas Air National Guard.

The problem was that the situation in Iraq refused to follow the script. As the war continued to grind on throughout the remainder of Bush's presidency, the premature 'Mission Accomplished' banner became an increasingly embarrassing symbol for his administration. The White House later claimed the banner had been the Navy's idea, but the Navy maintained the White House was to blame. It

Made in China?

must have been a self-hanging banner because no one would take responsibility for it.

And sometimes it's the little details that undermine the most carefully stage-managed event. In late January 2003 President Bush delivered a speech in the warehouse of JS Logistics, a St Louis trucking firm. The venue was chosen to highlight his proposed tax cuts that were supposed to benefit American small businesses. President Bush touted his plan in front of a screen that showed an enormous pile of boxes marked 'Made in USA', with real boxes from the warehouse stacked on either side of him. The setting was very pro-American business, very 'on message'. But reporters were curious about the brown packing tape they noticed on the boxes on either side of the president. The tape seemed to be concealing something. They peeled it back and found the phrase 'Made in China' beneath it. An embarrassed White House spokesperson blamed the cover-up on an anonymous volunteer who had prepped the area before the president's arrival. Whoever was responsible for the Potemkin Tape, the incident demonstrated that no matter how hard we try to fake reality, the truth inevitably finds a way of pushing back.

REALITY RULE 14.2
Tell a lie long enough, and some people might start to believe it.

Tina Brown, former editor of the *New Yorker*, once noted that many politicians subscribe to the 'as if' school of politics. They seem to believe that if they act *as if* everything is going well, eventually it will. Reality will conform to fantasy. Act as if the economy is strong, and it will be strong. Act as if a military campaign is succeeding, and it will succeed.

This philosophy seems to have been the inspiration behind the African-American Republican Leadership Council (AARLC), which came into existence in 2002. A significant problem faced by the American Republican party was that it attracted very few black voters. It rarely achieved more than 10–15 per cent of the black vote in any part of the country. And yet, anyone who stumbled across the AARLC wouldn't have thought this to be the case.

On its website the AARLC described itself as, 'The only nationwide conservative Republican organization dedicated to elect Reaganite pro-growth economic security African American Republicans to local, state, and the federal government.' It also declared itself committed to 'breaking the liberal Democrats' stranglehold over Black America' and emphasized its commitment to black leadership. Alongside this statement it displayed pictures of Ronald Reagan and George W. Bush.

It all sounded great, but in early 2003 *Washington Post* reporter Gene Weingarten did some research and discovered that exactly two of the organization's fifteen advisory panel members were black. The other thirteen were white. The 'Honorary Chairman' of the panel was black, but he had never heard of the group. All the candidates the AARLC supported in the November 2002 election were white. And an AARLC spokesman, whom Weingarten managed to reach by phone, admitted the organization's primary financial contributors were 'little old white ladies in Nebraska'. All of which begged the question: if the AARLC's leaders, supporters, and candidates were primarily white, wouldn't a better name for the group have been the Caucasian Republican Leadership Council? In fact, the AARLC appeared to have been an attempt by the Republican party to pretend that it did enjoy grassroots support from the black community, in the hope that if it pretended long enough, African-Americans might be persuaded to actually support it.

When it comes to pretending supporters into existence, the AARLC represents merely the tip of the iceberg. A vast industry works behind the scenes whose sole purpose is to create the illusion of popular support for political campaigns. It's known as the AstroTurf industry (since AstroTurf is a kind of fake grass, and this industry manufactures fake grassroots campaigns).

The way it works is that political operatives flood newspapers with letters designed to look as if they've been written by average citizens. This creates the phoney impression that there's a groundswell of support for whatever position the political hacks are trying to promote. For instance, in 2003

Democrats noticed similar letters in support of President Bush's economic policies appearing in papers such as the *Boston Globe*, the *Cincinnati Post*, and the *Fort Worth Star-Telegram*. The letters all started with the line: 'When it comes to the economy, President Bush is demonstrating genuine leadership.' The letter was traced back to a Republican website, gopteamleader.com, that had posted it and was encouraging readers to print it out and send it to local papers. Thus, an instant grassroots movement was created.

Political operatives of all persuasions use AstroTurf. Even animal-rights activists resorted to it to simulate support for a proposed amendment to Florida's constitution that would have granted rights to pregnant pigs. Nor are major corporations above employing it. In 1997, when the Justice Department sued Microsoft for violating antitrust laws, a vast citizens' movement seemed to rally spontaneously to the beleaguered corporation's defence. States' Attorneys General offices began receiving thousands of letters urging the government to get off the company's back. These outraged citizens even organized into pro-Microsoft groups with names such as Americans for Technology Leadership, Citizens Against Government Waste, and the Freedom to Innovate Network.

However, Utah Attorney General Mark Shurtleff became a little suspicious of this groundswell of support when he took a closer look at some of the pro-Microsoft letters he had received. He noticed they were peppered with similar phrases, such as 'strong competition and innovation have been the twin hallmarks of the technology industry' and 'the technology sector must remain free from excess regulation'. Also, some of the letters had arrived from non-existent towns such as 'Tucson, Utah' and, according to the voter rolls, a few had been sent by dead people. This meant one of two things: either a zombie army was rising up from the grave to defend the right of Microsoft to crush its competitors, or the grassroots campaign was phoney. Shurtleff guessed it was the latter, and he was right.

Some of the citizens' organizations turned out to be front groups created and funded by Microsoft. Paid PR grunts had composed the letters. Officials at these groups insisted they had then sent the letters to real people, who had forwarded them to their state officials, but somehow – the explanation was never very clear – a few of the letters had been forwarded by dead people living in non-existent places.

One potential danger for those who practise 'as if' politics is that the dividing line between fact and fiction can become dangerously blurred. Sometimes the politicians will come to believe their own fantasies. This creates the phenomenon of 'false memory syndrome'. Ronald Reagan, for example, liked to portray himself as a heroic figure, and eventually he came to believe this. He told several people, including Israeli Prime Minister Yitzhak Shamir and Simon Wiesenthal, that he had been present at the liberation of the Nazi death camps. The more mundane reality was that he had never been sent to Europe during World War II. He had spent the entire period in California making training films as part of the First Motion Picture Unit of the Army Air Corps.

Similarly, California Governor Arnold Schwarzenegger has insisted several times that the experience of watching the 1968 Nixon–Humphrey presidential debate on TV shortly after his arrival in America inspired him to enter politics and become a Republican. The problem with this story is that Nixon never debated Humphrey on TV.

The opposite of false memory syndrome is 'sudden

amnesia syndrome'. This is the inability to recall things of a potentially embarrassing or incriminating nature. Politicians often develop this condition when forced to participate in committee hearings or criminal investigations. Because, in the land of 'as if', if you deny a bad thing for long enough, it will eventually go away.

REALITY RULE 14.3
The money party always wins.

Cynics suggest that the modern political system in the United Kingdom and the United States is illusory in nature. They argue that although there appear to be differences between the major political parties, these differences mask the reality that, in fact, there is only one monolithic political party that has governed for centuries. It camouflages its monopoly on power by periodically reshuffling the face of government, hiring new actors to serve as presidents, senators, congressmen, and MPs. It is the Money Party.

If the political process is indeed a farce, as these cynics argue, then why not treat it as such? This line of thought has inspired a long-running tradition of satirical political campaigns.

The classic satirical campaign is that which seeks to elect 'Nobody' for president. Why elect Nobody? Because, his supporters answer, Nobody is the best candidate. Nobody cares. Nobody keeps his election promises. Nobody listens to your concerns. Nobody tells the truth. Nobody will defend your rights.

Nobody has run for President of the United States in every election since 1964, when journalist Arthur Hoppe first launched a campaign on his behalf. In 1975 comedian Wavy Gravy and Curtis Spangler took up Nobody's cause, hosting rallies for him across the country as the candidate of the Birthday Party. Their campaign continues at nobodyfor-president.org.

In 1959 there was a spirited campaign to elect Cacareco to the city council in Sao Paulo, Brazil. She won by a landslide. What made this unusual was that Cacareco was a five-year-old rhinoceros at the local zoo. Her election was widely viewed as a protest against the corruption of the local government. However, Cacareco didn't get to serve. Election officials nullified all her ballots, and a new election was held the following week.

Cacareco was not the first animal elected to public office. In 1936 the residents of Milton, Washington elected a mule named Boston Curtis to the post of Republican precinct committeeman. However, in Boston Curtis's case the voters were not aware of his mulish nature. Mayor Ken Simmons had surreptitiously taken the mule down to the courthouse and placed its hoof-print on all the documents necessary to register it to run. Simmons wanted to prove that most people blindly vote along party lines, especially when it comes to the lower-ranking offices on the ballot – meaning they'll vote for anyone, or anything, with the right political affiliation.

Britain's most famous satirical candidate is Screaming Lord Sutch. He campaigned in over forty elections and lost them all. The highest number of votes he ever received was 1,114 in the 1994 Rotherham by-election. However, he did earn a place in the *Guinness Book of World Records* as the parliamentary candidate who had stood more times than anyone else.

He first ran for a seat in parliament in 1963, at the age of twenty-two, as the candidate of the National Teenage Party with the slogan: 'Vote for Sutch and gain much.' In 1970 he switched his allegiance to the Go To Blazes Party before finally, in 1983, founding the Official Monster Raving Loony Party. As its candidate, his slogan was: 'Vote for insanity – you know it makes sense.' His proposals included bringing back the village idiot, putting joggers on treadmills to make them generate electricity, breeding fish in wine so they could be harvested ready-pickled, and making all dogs eat phosphorescent food so their poop could be seen at night.

Eventually British election officials started to raise the entry fee in the hope of preventing people such as Sutch from registering as candidates. However, Sutch simply paid the higher fees. He died in 1999, but the OMRLP lives on.

France's favourite satirical candidate is Ferdinand Lop. He was a writer, teacher, poet, street artist, and perennial candidate for the Presidency of the French Republic during the 1930s, '40s, and '50s. He advocated eliminating poverty (but only after 10 p.m.), extending the Boulevard St Michel to the English Channel with a comfort station every 50 yards, nationalizing brothels, providing an annual allowance to the widow of the Unknown Soldier, and relocating Paris to the countryside so that its residents could enjoy fresher air. He called this programme of reform 'Lopeotherapy'.

But perhaps the most eloquent of all the satirical candidates is the American who calls himself Vermin Supreme. He's repeatedly run for president on a platform that focuses almost entirely on dental hygiene, advocating 'government issued toothpaste containing addictive yet harmless substances; video surveillance through two way bathroom mirrors; electronic tracking, moisture and motion sensor devices in all toothbrushes . . . or even preventative dental maintenance detention facilities.' He notes, 'All politicians are, in fact, vermin. I am the Vermin Supreme; therefore I am the most qualified candidate.' This argument is difficult to counter.

REALITY RULE 14.4

'It's not who votes that counts; it's who counts the votes.'*

Hardly an election goes by that isn't marred by what are euphemistically termed 'voting irregularities'. Ranging from the trivial to the highly disturbing, these irregularities threaten both the legitimacy of the electoral process and our belief that our votes are being counted and might actually make a difference.

In 2002 self-described 'vote hackers' realized it was relatively easy to log on to the New Zealand Electoral Centre's website and edit existing information or add names to the voter rolls. The break-in was discovered when a woman received a letter from the centre asking her to confirm her name change from Fay to Fat Ass. Local papers also reported that 'a basset hound with prolific toilet habits' had been added as a voter. Its occupation was listed as 'cable layer'. Along similar lines, a farmer in Newmarket, England attempted to register her cows, Henry and Sophie Bull, as voters. She also tried to register her dog, Jake Woofles. But in a blow to the voting rights of animals, their applications were denied.

---

* Joseph Stalin, 1879–1953. (Whether Stalin actually said this is disputed, but no other source for the statement is known.)

Given such pranks, election officials are always on alert for obviously fake names such as Mary Poppins or Pippi Longstocking. Sometimes, however, they are over-vigilant. In 1996 an official in Quebec cried foul when he learned of a man registered to vote in his district who was named Omar Sharif and who supposedly lived with Martina Navratilova. Except in this case the son of the famous actor Omar Sharif really was living there with a stockbroker named Martina Navratilova.

The campaigns described above, though satirical, pay testament to the open, freewheeling spirit of democracy. However, democracy is not for everyone. Some can't stomach the prospect of a long and gruelling campaign that will end in almost certain disappointment. But there is another option for such people. They appoint themselves emperor.

This was Joshua Norton's strategy. On 17 September 1859 in a proclamation delivered to the *San Francisco Bulletin* he declared himself Emperor of the United States. For the rest of his life he dutifully performed his role as Emperor Norton I, walking the streets of San Francisco in a uniform completed by a plumed hat, gold epaulettes, and a sword. Crazy, perhaps, but in 1880 ten thousand people attended his funeral, and there is serious talk today of renaming San Francisco's Bay Bridge in his honour.

Then there was the Washington lawyer Russell Arundel, who in 1950 declared himself King of the Grand Principality of Outer Baldonia, a small rocky, uninhabited island off the coast of Nova Scotia that had formerly been known as Outer Bald Tusket. The Outer Baldonian Declaration of Independence included 'the inalienable right to lie and be believed; to drink, swear, and gamble; to sleep all day and stay up all night'. The tiny principate entered into international diplomacy on 9 March 1953 when it declared war on the Soviet Union. Happily for both sides, the Soviet Union chose not to fight.

Finally, taking up Emperor Norton's mantle in the present is Los Angeles resident HRM Caesar St Augustine de Buonaparte (that is his preferred title). In the 1990s Buonaparte sent President Clinton a letter declaring war on the United States. Buonaparte claims that Clinton's failure to respond means the United States implicitly conceded defeat. Therefore, Buonaparte is now Emperor of the United States. All hail Emperor Buonaparte!

More disturbing are the rigged elections. The most legendary bogus election occurred in 1927 when Charles King was elected president of Liberia with over 240,000 votes cast for him – in a population with only 15,000 registered voters. The *Guinness Book of World Records* named this election the most fraudulent in world history – but that was before witnessing the Iraqi election of 2002, in which Saddam Hussein received 11 million votes without a single vote cast against him.

Officials monitoring American elections regularly catch a wide range of attempted fraud. During the 2004 presidential election this included voter registration cards completed in suspiciously similar handwriting, cards submitted with non-existent addresses, and cards filled out by people who had been dead for twenty years. Someone even tried to obtain absentee ballots on behalf of an entire neighbourhood – everyone in it, by coincidence, was apparently going to be out of town on election day. These were just the cases that got noticed.

Electronic touch-screen voting technology has created entirely new possibilities for vote rigging. Although the backers of this technology assure everyone it's foolproof, detractors warn that a few keystrokes could replace entire ballot counts with phoney tallies, and no paper trail would record the deception. People would believe they were voting, while in reality the vote count was being manufactured by a hacker thousands of miles away.

Ultimately we rely on the media to watch over the integrity of the electoral process and inform us of suspicious activity, but the media is often distracted by a more important agenda: attracting viewers and getting a scoop.

In order to attract viewers, the media needs drama. To squeeze this out of elections (which often aren't that thrilling), journalists resort to 'horse-race' reporting. Elections become competitions in which the focus is on who happens to be slightly ahead in the polls at any one moment, rather than on what the actual issues are that candidates are debating.

This was taken to a ridiculous extreme in March 2004 when Taiwanese audiences sat glued to their sets watching real-time presidential election results flash across their screens. TV commentators reported the election just like a sporting event: 'More vote numbers are now coming in . . . The figures are jumping faster and faster . . . The election outcome is getting unpredictable at every minute.' On some channels opposition candidate Lien Chan took an early and commanding lead; other stations had incumbent Chen Shui-bian ahead. But it didn't really matter which channel a viewer watched because the election committee hadn't actually released any figures. The stations were inventing the numbers out of thin air.

Instead of inventing numbers, the American media usually relies on a complex system of exit polls and statistical analysis to predict results. The problem is that media organizations are often so eager to get a scoop by being the first to call an election, that they jump the gun and make bad calls. The most notorious case of this occurred in November 1948 when the *Chicago Tribune* ran a bold-faced headline declaring 'DEWEY DEFEATS TRUMAN'. When it realized its mistake, it desperately tried to pull the papers from newsstands, but it was too late. A copy had already made its way to the actual winner of the election, Truman, who posed for a photo that became famous, showing him holding the erroneous newspaper above his head. Truman later had the headline made into a paperweight he kept in the Oval Office.

More recently, in 2000 networks first called the election for Gore, then said it was too close to call, then said Bush was the winner before finally saying, again, that it was too close to call. In 2004 the networks were more cautious, but still got bitten when exit polls seemed to show a Kerry win, though Bush walked away with the victory. (Conspiracy theorists speculated that the exit polls were right, and it was the official election results that were made up.) All the networks got it right in 2008, but then Obama made it easy for them by winning in a landslide.

REALITY RULE 14.5

In politics it doesn't matter if an accusation is true or false, only that it sticks.

Political campaigners don't like to leave anything to chance, especially in a close race. To make sure their candidate has an edge, they'll readily lie or cheat. Such tactics are known as 'dirty tricks'. Like voting irregularities, they range from the light-hearted to the low-down and despicable.

The twentieth-century master of the light-hearted dirty trick was Dick Tuck, whose target of choice was Richard Nixon. In 1956 Tuck hired dump trucks to drive past the site of the GOP Convention in San Francisco where Nixon was running as Eisenhower's vice president. The trucks had the words 'Dump Nixon' painted on their sides. He followed this up in 1968 by hiring pregnant women to attend Nixon rallies carrying signs that read 'Nixon's The One'. But Tuck's most famous stunt (which some argue may be an urban legend promoted by Tuck himself) was dressing up as a conductor and signalling a train to leave the station as Nixon was delivering a speech from the caboose. Tuck's antics drove Nixon so crazy that Nixon eventually told an aide that the Republicans needed to develop a 'Dick Tuck capability' of their own.

Similar efforts continue today. In 2004 Democratic pranksters engineered it so that if you typed 'miserable failure' into Google, President Bush's biography was the first thing to come up. Republican pranksters responded by making sure John Kerry's website was the first hit when anyone searched for the word 'waffles' (a reference to the allegation that Kerry waffled on important issues).

Unfortunately, most dirty tricks are not so harmless. Many involve character assassination, that art of insinuation whereby politicians accuse each other (usually through proxies) of all manner of vice and sin, regardless of proof.

Character assassination is a time-honoured political tradition. Aaron Burr was defeated in New York's 1804 gubernatorial campaign in large part due to an accusation that he frequented brothels. The *American Citizen* claimed to have a list of twenty prostitutes willing to declare he was their favourite customer. In 1844 the opponents of James Polk, furious they couldn't find dirt on the squeaky-clean Democratic presidential candidate, invented a story about how 'Baron von Roorback' had encountered a group of Polk's beaten and abused slaves while travelling through America. In reality, neither the slaves nor Baron von Roorback existed. Throughout the remainder of the nineteenth century, the term 'roorback' was used as slang meaning to smear with false charges.

The modern-day equivalent of the term 'roorback' is 'swift boat'. It refers to the organization Swift Boat Veterans for Truth, founded to oppose John Kerry's 2004 presidential bid. Members of this group alleged Kerry faked injuries while serving as a commander of a swift boat in Vietnam in order to receive a purple heart. However, they had no proof to support this allegation, and the veterans who actually served with Kerry emphatically denied it. Nevertheless, the controversy proved a distraction to Kerry's campaign, which doubtless was its intended purpose. The term 'to swift boat' then entered into popular usage. When rumours spread during the 2008 election alleging that Barack Obama was a secret Muslim, Democrats complained that he was being swift-boated.

Fake photographs are a favourite of political dirty tricksters. In 1950 Millard Tydings (a US Senator from Maryland) challenged Senator Joseph McCarthy by calling his allegation that hundreds of communists were working in the State Department 'a fraud, a hoax, and a deceit'. As payback, McCarthy's staff faked a picture showing Tydings apparently chatting with Earl Browder, head of the American Communist Party. They disseminated this photo shortly before a senate race in which Tydings was running against John Butler. The image is believed to have contributed to Tydings's defeat.

A similar guilt-by-association-themed picture circulated online during the 2004 presidential campaign. It showed John Kerry sharing the stage at an anti-Vietnam peace rally with Jane Fonda – Fonda being the bête noire of pro-war conservatives because of a trip to North Vietnam she made in 1972. However, the scene never occurred in real life. Photographer Ken Light recognized the image as one he had taken in 1971 at a Peace Rally in Long Island, but his original picture had shown Kerry sitting alone. Not only had Fonda not been anywhere in the shot, she hadn't even attended the rally.

Of the many fake political photos that circulated during the 2008 campaign, a particularly popular one, mistakenly believed by many to be real, showed Obama casually smoking a cigarette. Obama has admitted to being a smoker, though he has been trying to quit. (By his own admission, he has had a few lapses.) Nevertheless, there are hardly any photos of him smoking, largely because his campaign made enormous efforts to stop such photos getting out, fearing negative public reaction. In the photo in question, an unknown hoaxer had digitally inserted the cigarette into Obama's mouth.

In discussions of dirty-trick campaigns people sometimes refer to two particular varieties of chicanery: black propaganda and grey propaganda. Black propaganda refers to material produced by one side in a conflict that has been designed to make it appear as if the other side was the source. The material is usually of an embarrassing or incriminating nature. For example, in November 2003 flyers advertising a Young Democrats' rally for Democratic candidate Howard Dean appeared on the Dartmouth College campus. The flyers were decorated with an image of the Confederate flag, making it appear as if Dean was trying to reach out to Confederate

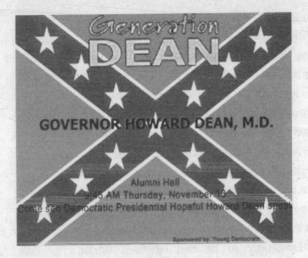

Confederates for Howard Dean.

sympathizers in the New England area. (Dean *had* recently remarked that he wanted to be 'the candidate for guys with Confederate flags in their pickup trucks'.) However, the Young Democrats had nothing to do with the flyer. It was black propaganda created by their opponents.

Grey propaganda is similar to black propaganda, except it is disguised to appear to come from a neutral, objective source. For example, in 2004 a chart began to circulate online showing that American states whose populations possessed on average higher incomes and IQs voted for Gore in the 2000 presidential elections, whereas their poorer, dumber counterparts voted for Bush. The implication was that smart people vote Democratic, whereas stupid people vote Republican. The source of this chart was said to be an academic book titled *IQ and the Wealth of Nations* by Richard Lynn and Tatu Vanhanen. Both the *St Petersburg Times* and *The Economist* printed the chart as fact. But in reality the chart had never appeared in Lynn and Vanhanen's book. Its true source was someone who used the screen name Robert Calvert to post it to a Mensa newsgroup in 2002. He had invented the data.

In some instances grey propaganda actually consists of accurate information. For instance, during the Cold War the Soviet Union covertly disseminated pictures that highlighted racial tension in the United States. The images were real, but their use was misleading because viewers weren't aware of who was circulating them. This suggests a footnote should be added to the golden rule of hoax-busting (that information is only as good as its source). The rule is true, but it is complicated by the fact that very often the source is not who it appears to be.

Reality Check

Question 1. The residents of the Ecuadorian town of Picoazá once chose a foot powder named Pulvapies as their mayor. True or false?

Question 2. This picture shows the German dictator Adolf Hitler as a baby. True or false?

ANSWERS

1. In 1967 the residents of Picoazá did elect Pulvapies foot powder as their mayor. In the run-up to municipal elections throughout Ecuador, the Pulvapies foot powder company had launched an advertising campaign that featured the slogan: 'Vote for any candidate, but if you want hygiene, vote for Pulvapies'. Immediately before the election it also distributed thousands of leaflets which read 'For Mayor: Honourable Pulvapies'. The leaflets were the same size and colour as official voting papers. Residents of the small town of Picoazá apparently took the advice to heart because a majority of them wrote 'Honourable Pulvapies' on their ballots, making the foot powder their new mayor. It was not clear whether the election of the foot powder was intended as a protest vote, or if it was an indication of poor literacy skills in the region (i.e. many people might have thought Pulvapies was a genuine, human candidate).

2. The photo of 'baby Adolf' surfaced in 1933 and was distributed by Acme Newspictures to all its subscribers. As a consequence, it ran in many American and British newspapers. However, the photo was not real. The photo actually showed an American child, John May Warren, son of Mrs Harriet Downs of Ohio. A hoaxer had somehow obtained the photo (it is not clear how) and darkened the child's features to make him appear more menacing. The photo could be considered an example of grey propaganda since it appeared to come from a neutral, objective source, and yet it was clearly designed to sway popular opinion against the German dictator.

FIFTEEN

Death

Determining when someone is dead would seem like it should be a matter-of-fact issue. They're either dead or they're not. But as with everything else in the modern world, once lawyers and doctors get involved, everything becomes far more ambiguous. Protracted legal battles have been fought over the definition of death, particularly in cases involving donor organs. Once you add hoaxers into this mix, things start to get really strange.

REALITY RULE 15.1

For some, death is merely a career move.

Feeling depressed? Weighed down by debt and obligations? Looking to start over with a clean slate? Have no fear. There's a solution to all your problems. Just fake your death. It's the 'Get out of jail free' card of life. People do it all the time.

A popular non-messy way of checking out (without really checking out) is to forge a death certificate. What people who choose this method often forget, however, is that once they're officially dead they need to stay dead, which means under the radar. Inevitably, after living for a few years with a new identity, they get arrested for a minor offence, the police check their fingerprints, and the game is up. In 1997 William Peterson filed a death certificate for himself rather than face up to a drunk-driving charge, and he spent the next eight years living carefree as William Arksey . . . until he was arrested for forgery. At his trial Arksey/Peterson pleaded for mercy, telling the judge his criminal life was in the past and noting, 'I was a different person then.' Despite the obvious truth of this statement, the judge was not sympathetic.

Another strategy is to go missing. This is particularly popular among those with an accomplice, such as a spouse, who can claim any life insurance due. But again, a major challenge is to remain under the radar. The dead person must sever all ties with their former life in order to avoid being seen by those who believe him dead. This is harder than it might sound. Those in hiding often develop an overwhelming urge to see their friends and family again.

John Darwin provided a recent example of this phenomenon. He went canoeing off the coast of Hartlepool in March 2002 and never returned. Three weeks later the remains of his canoe washed onshore. The authorities presumed he was dead. In reality he was hiding in his wife's apartment and later in Panama. His wife collected £250,000 in insurance money. But after five years John decided he missed his sons and staged a dramatic return to London, showing up in a West End police station claiming he had no memory of the past five years. His wife acted overjoyed to see him. This ruse was foiled when recent pictures of him and his wife together in Panama surfaced on the Internet.

It used to be that the most convincing method of staging

your death was to leave a dead body behind. However, modern forensic techniques, such as DNA analysis, have made this much harder to pull off. At the very least a would-be death-faker needs a body that's an approximate match to his own – of the same gender, height, and weight. It was the weight that gave Joseph Kalady away after he killed a handyman in 2001, disguised the victim's body as his own, and did a runner. Kalady weighed over 450 pounds, and the dead body did not, so the police knew something was fishy. The police arrested Kalady two years later, but while being held awaiting trial he eluded justice a second time by dying. This time it was for real (or so the police believe).

Some people fake their death not to collect insurance money or evade the law, but simply to watch others grieve them. This is particularly popular online where it's possible to kill off your online persona and then rubberneck at your own virtual funeral.

11 September brought a glut of fake online deaths as people tried to look like instant heroes (or tragic victims) in the eyes of their computer friends. One person's elaborate ruse convinced many on the LiveJournal community that he had died rushing into the burning World Trade Center to save people. The outpouring of grief and commiseration that followed turned to disgust when the hoax was exposed.

The phoney online suicide, announced in advance, is also a guaranteed attention-getter. One joker's 'countdown to oblivion' weblog declared he would take his own life in a few days: 'My name is Jerry Romero, and I am 23 years old,' he wrote. 'On January 13th, I am going to kill myself.' Much virtual hand-wringing and pleading to reconsider ensued, but when 13 January arrived visitors to his site were met with a single word: PWNED.

If you can't stomach the thought of faking your own death, you can always fake someone else's. Why would you do this? Two reasons: to get sympathy (and thereby financial help), or as a prank.

After 9/11 Maureen Curry of Vancouver, Canada reported her daughter killed in the terrorist attack, and complained her employer had refused her request for bereavement leave. Friends and politicians quickly raised over $2,000 for her, only to learn her daughter was alive and well and living in Winnipeg, though the two had been estranged for years. Likewise, Cyril Kendall's report that his son Wilfred had died in the World Trade Center netted him $160,000 in compensation from the Red Cross. There was just one problem: he didn't have a son named Wilfred. But he did have a shiny new car thanks to the Red Cross money. He subsequently lost the car when he was thrown into jail for thirty-three years.

As for the False Death Claim Prank, it was pioneered by eighteenth-century satirists such as Jonathan Swift and Benjamin Franklin. Both publicly predicted the deaths of famous astrologers and then declared their predictions had come true – much to the annoyance of the astrologers who were very much alive.

In modern times, anonymous online jokers are usually responsible for fake-death pranks. Their targets are typically entertainers. In fact, a good indication of a celebrity's star power is the number of times her death has been falsely reported. By this measure Britney Spears is the most popular star, since rumours of her death via car crash have circulated numerous times online. Paris Hilton comes in a close second with reports of having been stabbed in jail and committed suicide. Another faux news report claimed Hilton had expressed a desire to be cryogenically frozen after death with her dogs Tinkerbell and Cinderella. Michael Jackson ranks third, with multiple reported suicide attempts to his credit.

The opposite of faking your death is to die but have no one believe you're really dead. This has been the fate of a number of celebrities. It's not clear why some celebrity deaths inspire death-hoax rumours while others don't, but once a rumour takes hold it can have amazing staying power. And no celebrity clings more stubbornly to life after death than Elvis Presley.

The official story is that Presley died on 16 August 1977. The unofficial story is that the corpse in his coffin was a wax dummy, and no body was buried in the meditation garden at Graceland. As his loyal fans argue, if Elvis was buried at Graceland why does his tombstone misspell his name? The correct spelling is 'Elvis Aron Presley', but the name on the grave is 'Elvis Aaron Presley'. Why the extra 'a'? Does it stand for 'alive'? Inquiring minds want to know.

Some say Elvis went into the Federal Witness Protection programme after getting mixed up with the mob. Others say he decided to do a runner after getting tired of the pressures of stardom. Still others insist he was abducted by aliens. In any case, people keep seeing him all over the place: pumping gas in the Australian outback; eating cheeseburgers in St Paul, Minnesota; or ordering double lattes in Pensacola, Florida.

In 2002 psychiatrist Donald Hinton published a book in which he claimed he had been treating Elvis for back pain since 1997. According to Hinton, Elvis called it quits in 1977 because of his failing health and took up a more stress-free life under the name Jesse, in honour of his still-born twin brother. He lived in Apopka, Florida for a while before settling in Missouri. Hinton promised Elvis would return to public life on the twenty-fifth anniversary of his death, but Elvis apparently developed a case of last-minute jitters because he pulled a no-show.

Another star who refuses to remain dead is Jim Morrison, lead singer of The Doors. He supposedly died of a heart attack (or a heroin overdose) in Paris on 3 July 1971. But businessman Gerald Pitts claims he found Jim 'living on a ranch in the Pacific Northwest in the summer of 1998'. Apparently the singer had tired of the celebrity rat-race and decided to become a gun-toting cowboy. Pitts will tell you all about it in a video he sells for $24.95.

And then there's rap star Tupac Shakur. Was he really killed in a drive-by shooting on 7 September 1996? A group of sceptics who call themselves 'Seven-Day Theorists' (the name is inspired by clues Tupac supposedly left in his final album, *The Don Killuminati: The Seven Day Theory*) argue the rapper faked his death with a plan to 'resurrect' himself after seven years. His death's seventh anniversary passed without incident, which put a dent in that theory. But in April 2005 a fake CNN news story raced around the Internet claiming Tupac had shown up to do a little shopping at some high-end stores in Beverly Hills. He mustn't have found anything he liked, because he hasn't been seen since.

To date, no celebrity has justified death-hoax rumours by returning from the grave. The closest we have come to this was the faux return of comedian Andy Kaufman. During his life Kaufman often talked of faking his death. He joked that if he ever did 'pull an Elvis' he would return twenty years later to tell everyone about it. Then he died of lung cancer on 16 May 1984. Or did he? On 16 May 2004, a press release announced his return and a blog apparently authored by him appeared online. Where had he been hiding out? On New

York City's Upper West Side, said the resurrected Kaufman. A buzz of Internet speculation ensued. Had Kaufman really pulled off the greatest hoax in history? Sadly, no. After several weeks the joke got old for whoever was behind it (we still don't know their identity), and new posts stopped appearing on Andy's blog.

Perhaps celebrities never return from the grave because death is so lucrative for them. In fact, death doesn't even put a dent in the productivity of many artists. Tupac Shakur has released seven albums since dying, which may explain why so many people think he's still alive. Jimi Hendrix has produced hundreds of albums post-mortem, compared to just three pre-mortem. Ernest Hemingway publishes a new work every few years, decades after his demise. And Robert Ludlum has authored half-a-dozen thrillers since giving up the ghost.

These artists manage to pull off this trick because works they partially completed while alive – experimental studio sessions or unfinished stories – are polished up by others and unloaded on the public. Far more remarkable are the entirely new works some artists create while dead. One of the more notorious examples of this phenomenon is gothic novelist Virginia Andrews, who has churned out bestsellers ever since dying in 1986. The books are actually written by a ghost-writer, Andrew Niederman, who claims to be channelling her creative spirit (which gives a literal spin on being a ghostwriter). Occasionally Niederman even makes publicity appearances as Andrews (not in drag, as far as I know). However, this bait-and-switch was not made clear to Andrews's fans until years after her death. Niederman's name didn't appear on the books, and the publisher implied (falsely) that Andrews had largely completed these novels before her death. Even today many people continue to buy Andrews's books, believing they were actually written by her.

Which goes to show that, just as the ancient Greeks believed no one was fully dead as long as they lived on in the memories of the living, in the modern world no one is fully dead as long as there's money to be made out of them.

Reality Check

Question 1. Arizona police reported finding a 1967 Chevy Impala embedded in the side of a cliff in the middle of the desert. Apparently its owner, in an attempt to break the land-speed record, had bolted a solid-fuel rocket to the roof of his car. He activated the rocket on a deserted stretch of highway, causing the car to rapidly gain a speed in excess of 300 miles per hour. When it hit a bump, it flew into the air and then into the cliff, killing the driver instantly. True or false?

Question 2. A New Jersey real estate development company operates a chain of cemetery theme parks where visitors can dine at fine restaurants, shop, and go on rides in addition to visiting their loved ones' graves. True or false?

Question 3. The Preserve A Life company will freeze-dry and mount the body of your loved one, allowing you to keep the body permanently on display in your home. True or false?

Question 4. Because of a shortage of trained bugle players, the American military has developed a 'push-button bugle' for use during military funerals. The soldier who plays it merely has to flip a switch, put the instrument to his lips, and maintain that pose as an electronic chip plays a recorded version of the memorial music. True or false?

Question 5. A man was once killed by heating a lava lamp on a stove. True or false?

Question 6. A British woman was once killed while strolling across a park by a shaft of frozen urine falling from a plane's leaky toilet. True or false?

Question 7. A German man once arranged to have his body fed to piranhas after he died. True or false?

Question 8. A loving husband once preserved his wife's body in an airtight glass container that he now uses as a coffee table. True or false?

Question 9. There is a company that promises to turn the cremated remains of your loved one into a diamond. True or false?

Question 10. A Finnish phone company once offered a service that allowed customers to send a prayer to Jesus via text message. True or false?

Question 11. The Afterlife Telegram Service maintains a team of terminally ill patients who promise, for a fee of $5 per word, to memorize any message you want to send to someone in the great beyond, and to deliver it personally when they reach the other side. True or false?

ANSWERS

1. For many years the story of 'Rocket Man' circulated on the Internet and was believed to be true. The tale's popularity helped launch the concept of giving 'Darwin Awards' to people whose extreme poor judgement resulted in their deaths (their stupidity deselecting them from the gene pool – making them examples of Charles Darwin's theory of natural selection). However, the Arizona Department of Public Safety has no record of anyone dying in such a fashion. In other words, the story is an urban legend.

2. In March 1999 ads announcing the imminent launch of a 'Final Curtain' cemetery theme park chain appeared in a variety of magazines. Its motto was, 'Death got you down? At last an alternative!' Numerous newspapers and TV stations (including the *New York Daily News*, the *Boston Herald*, and Fox TV) reported this unusual cemetery concept. However, the media had been taken in by prankster Joey Skaggs, who later explained that he perpetrated the hoax in order to draw attention to the death-care industry, which he described as 'a giant corporate scam, exquisitely successful at commercializing death'.

3. The Preserve A Life company was the subject of an October 2004 spoof article in the *Phoenix New Times*. The article claimed the company had pioneered the art of 'Humidermy' (human taxidermy) that allowed the permanent preservation of bodies in posed positions. 'Children have been posed on bicycles and skateboards, grandmothers in rocking chairs, and grandfathers playing boccie ball.' Many people did not recognize the article as a spoof and were taken in by it.

4. The American military has recently begun to run out of trained bugle players, and its solution was to invent a 'push-button bugle'. The introduction of these phoney bugles inspired some veterans to create Bugles Across America, a network of volunteer buglers who fill in at funerals when military buglers aren't available. But even this effort can't make up for the bugler shortfall. So push-button bugles remain in frequent use at services. The push-button bugles

play a version of taps performed by US Army Sgt Maj. Woodrow 'Woody' English, who is still alive. This places him in the unique position that someday he may play taps at his own funeral.

5. True. In November 2004 Philip Quinn of Kent, Washington heated a lava lamp on a stove in an attempt to make it bubble faster, only to have the lamp explode and spray out shards of glass, one of which punctured his heart and killed him. His parents found his body in his trailer home. Police stated no drugs or alcohol were in his system when he died. Apparently he just wanted to know what a really hot lava lamp would look like. Call it a case of 'curiosity killed the lava-lamp owner'.

6. False. *The Day Today*, a spoof news programme that aired in Britain during the 1990s, ran a brief segment about a woman who died in this fashion. The story was a joke, but an accompanying picture of a woman lying on Wandsworth Common, a large urine icicle lodged in her side, made its way onto the Internet and has circulated there ever since.

7. False. A man tried to do this, but he didn't succeed. In 2004, German artist Karl Friedrich Lentze read about a Dutch man who requested his body be fed to snails after his death. This inspired him to write to various zoos to inquire whether they would feed his corpse to piranhas. He suggested the event would serve an educational purpose. The director of the Cologne Zoo responded that piranhas prefer live flesh, so Lentze would really have to be fed to them while he was alive. Lentze demurred, but did propose the zoo staff poke his dead body with a stick to make it look like he was moving. The director didn't think this would work, which put an end to the piranha funeral.

8. A picture that has circulated widely on the Internet shows a man enjoying a beer with a friend, oblivious to a woman lying in the glass case upon which his beer is resting. The attached story tells of Jeff, who – unable to bear the thought that his young wife Lucy had died – preserved her body in an airtight glass case that he now uses as a coffee table. In reality a body couldn't be preserved this easily. It would soon begin to decay. Lenin's body has been displayed in a glass case for years, but it requires constant maintenance by a team of embalmers. The 'dead wife as coffee table' story is a decades-old urban legend. The picture circulating on the Internet, taken by an unknown photographer, seems to be an attempt to recreate it.

9. True. The company is called LifeGem, and it is real. Its website promises 'a certified, high quality diamond created from the carbon of your loved one as a memorial to their unique and wonderful life'. Prices range from $2,500 to $14,000. The bodies have to be cremated first (so don't deliver Uncle Joe's corpse straight to the company's door), but LifeGem happily accepts animal cremains as well. Your pet hamster can be with you forever, on a ring around your finger.

10. True. A Finnish phone company did offer this service. What made this particularly interesting is that the company also promised Jesus would respond. To test the service, a Finnish newspaper sent a prayer for help. Jesus came back with this cryptic reply, 'unless you follow God's will much better than priests and pharaohs, you will not be allowed into the heavenly kingdom'. The phone company eventually discontinued the service after receiving numerous complaints.

11. True. This service does exist. Or rather, it did as of 2003. It may have since folded from a lack of customers, one of its only paying clients being a *Washington Post* reporter who wanted to send a rude message to Adolf Hitler. It was the creation of Paul Kinsella of New Athens, Illinois. He acknowledged many things could go wrong with the delivery of the message, and so his service offered few guarantees. For instance, Kinsella noted, 'Reincarnation could cause a problem', and also, 'If the afterlife is segregated into heaven, hell and purgatory, it is possible that the messenger will not be sent to the same place as the addressee.' However, if the messenger did not die within the year, the client received their money back. All proceeds went to charity, or towards the messenger's medical expenses.

GLOSSARY: Some Other Things To Look Out For

Ambush Marketing, v. Purposefully undermining a marketing campaign. Example: in 1998 the Coca-Cola Bottling Co. sponsored a 'Coke in Education Day' in Columbia County, Georgia. The corporation offered $500 to the school that staged the most creative Coke promotion. Officials at Greenbrier High gathered students outside to spell 'Coke' for a photograph, with executives from Coca-Cola watching. Just as the picture was taken, one of the students, Mike Cameron, took off his shirt to reveal a Pepsi T-shirt. The stunt ruined the picture and got Mike suspended, but it made him a legend among those who love to undermine corporate marketing efforts.

Beer Goggle Effect, n. Alcohol's ability to make people seem better looking than they are. A 2002 study by Glasgow University psychology professor Barry Jones found that after drinking two pints of beer people were 25 per cent more likely than those who had drunk nothing to find faces of the opposite sex attractive.

Brainwashington, n. The propaganda-fed version of reality that emanates from the Washington establishment. (Citation: Mathias Broeckers, 'Welcome to Brainwashington', Lecture at the Chaos Communication Camp, 9 August 2003.)

Botox Mask, n. The blank, emotionless expression that results from the overuse of Botox, a bacterial toxin that smoothes out wrinkles by temporarily paralysing facial muscles. Victims gaze out with an eerie wax-museum stare no matter what emotional situation they encounter: comedy, grief, or tragedy. Also referred to as a 'Botox permagrin'.

Celebrity Worship Syndrome, n. An obsessive fascination with the lives of the rich and famous. Psychologists speculate that people who exhibit this syndrome have difficulty forming real relationships with those around them and therefore form imaginary relationships with people they see on screen.

Credibility Gap, n. The difference between what politicians say and what they actually do. The term became popular during the Vietnam War when soldiers would frequently speak of being 'ambushed at credibility gap'.

CSI Effect, n. The belief that all criminal cases are solved using the high-tech, forensic science seen on TV crime shows such as *CSI*. Lawyers have noticed that the lack of such high-tech evidence can seriously prejudice a jury against a prosecutor's case. This is a manifestation of the pervasive 'if it's not like what we see on TV then it can't be real' mentality.

Death By Sims, n. The result of the decision to kill off the character that symbolically represents you in a Sims game.

Disinformation Campaign, n. The deliberate planting of false information (often by government agencies) in order to sway public opinion, either at home or abroad.

Dorian Gray Syndrome, n. A psychiatric disorder characterized by an obsessive desire to maintain the appearance of youth. A refusal to accept the reality of growing older. Named after Oscar Wilde's character who remains young while his portrait ages. (Citation: *Intl. Journal of Clinical Pharmacology and Therapeutics*, Vol. 39, No. 7/2001, 279–83.)

Dorito Syndrome, n. A lingering sense of dissatisfaction and emptiness caused by prolonged exposure to things with little nutritional or edifying content: junk food, video games, the Internet, etc.

Doublespeak, n. Language that pretends to convey information, but actually conceals or distorts it. Example: referring to the unemployed as 'job-seekers' or to civilian casualties of war as 'collateral damage'. Derives from the term 'newspeak', coined by George Orwell in his novel *1984*.

Drink the Kool-Aid, v. To adopt a belief unquestioningly. Often used in the negative as an imperative: 'Don't drink the Kool-Aid!' Refers to the members of the Jim Jones cult who committed mass suicide in 1978 by drinking cyanide-laced Kool-Aid. However, according to Kool-Aid enthusiasts, the members of Jones' People's Temple actually drank Flavor-Aid, which is a cheap imitation.

Elvis Spotting, n. A sighting of someone who is supposed to be dead, but who is walking around in public.

Emulator, n. A consumer who buys products, such as sneakers, in order to fantasize about being someone else such as the basketball star Michael Jordan, i.e. 'I want to be like Mike.'

Faux-lebrity, n. A star of a reality TV show who is well known enough to be recognized, but who will never attain the status or commercial appeal of a true celebrity. Also known as a 'surface celebrity'.

Faux-mosexuality, n. Homosexuality faked in order to appear trendy.

First-Season Syndrome, n. A theorized pattern on reality shows whereby only the first season is real (in the sense of being unscripted and spontaneous). In subsequent seasons players are aware of the show's format and possible strategies and therefore no longer display genuine reactions, but merely play to audience expectations.

Framing, n. The belief that an experience isn't real until it's been 'framed' by a camera. **v.** Photographing every moment of a vacation (or event), as if having a photo of yourself grinning in front of the Taj Mahal, Eiffel Tower, or Big Ben somehow makes the experience of being there genuine.

Frankenfood, n. Food that comes from genetically modified plants or animals. Artificially engineered food.

Fraud Frond, n. A mobile phone transmission tower disguised as a tree. There are reportedly over 30,000 of them in the United States alone, as many cities require mobile phone antennas to be disguised.

Frequent Liar Miles, n. What people earn by lying frequently. Politicians tend to accrue a lot of them. (Possible first usage: 4 August 2000 in the *San Francisco Chronicle* to describe the many air miles logged by candidates during the presidential campaign.)

Friend of a Friend, n. The source of information in many bogus tales. Example: 'I know this is true because it happened to a friend of a friend,' an email might begin before launching into a story about two lovers in a car terrorized by a serial killer with a hook for a hand. Often abbreviated as FOAF.

George Spelvin, n. A name used in movie credits and theatre bills to disguise the fact that an actor is playing dual roles. The tradition of using this name dates back to 1906. In the 1970s a porn star had a career as Georgina Spelvin.

Ghost Voting, v. Voting on legislative measures while not physically present. Typically a lawmaker achieves this trick by jamming the 'yea' or 'nay' button at his desk to hold it down. The button racks up a perfect voting record and the legislator gets paid a per diem for being there to vote, even if he was actually on vacation. In one notorious case in Pennsylvania a button held down by a paperclip cast the deciding vote on a divisive 1991 tax bill.

Greenscamming, n. Deceptively using environmentally friendly rhetoric for non- or anti-environmental purposes. Example: the organization Concerned Alaskans for Resources and Environment may sound green, but its purpose is to lobby for the expansion of clear-cut logging permits.

Half-People, n. People who become so accustomed to presenting an image or caricature of themselves in public that they're eventually reduced to caricature in private life as well. An occupational hazard of being a celebrity. Coined by Andy Warhol.

Hyperreality, n. The kind of reality fake things acquire when they become valued for their own sake, not merely as substitutes for real things. In the words of Umberto Eco, when they become 'authentic fakes'. Example: Disneyland is often described as hyperreal because it contains many simulations of other places (the African rainforest, Main Street USA, etc.), and yet the simulations are interesting in their own right and not merely as substitutes for something else.

Identity Hacking, v. Supplying false information when asked online for details about your identity. Studies show people routinely lie when asked for personal information on Internet surveys or when required to register in order to view content on a site.

Image Aspirations, n. The amount of appearance-altering surgery a person is willing, or would like, to have. Typically the major constraint on such aspirations is the size of the person's bank account.

Imagined Ugliness, n. The irrational, obsessive belief that a body part is deformed. Also known as body dysmorphic disorder. Sufferers of this condition seek out cosmetic surgery, repeatedly, to correct the perceived flaw. (Citation: K A Phillips, et al., 'Body dysmorphic disorder: 30 cases of imagined ugliness', *Am J Psychiatry*, 1993; 150:302–8.)

In Silico, adj. Describing an experiment conducted by means of a computer simulation, as opposed to in vitro (in a test tube, or a lab), or in vivo (in a living creature).

In the Plastic Closet, adj. Where you are if you've had plastic surgery but are unwilling to admit it.

Just-Add-Water Celebrity, n. An instant celebrity created by marketing hype. Typically lacking in the qualities – such as talent, charisma, wealth, or family name – whereby other celebrities earn their fame. Examples include the stars of many reality TV shows.

Karaoke Culture, n. A society in which imitation passes for reality and originality is non-existent. Derives from a statement by Malcolm McLaren, former manager of the Sex Pistols: 'Today we live in a karaoke world. A world without any particular point of view . . . liberated by hindsight, unencumbered by the messy process of creativity, and free from any real responsibility beyond the actual performance.'

Kodak Courage, n. An exaggerated sense of courage caused by the presence of a camera. The extreme behaviour people wouldn't engage in if they weren't being filmed.

La Malbouffe, **n.** A French term for fake food. Coined by the farmer José Bové, who became a national hero for burning down a McDonald's restaurant in Millau. He claimed McDonald's fast food was corrupting French culture.

Liar's Remorse, n. The sense of guilt that haunts people who have told a lie. Noticeably absent among politicians.

McJob, n. A dead-end job, typically in the service sector of the economy. Lacks the features real jobs used to provide, such as benefits or the potential for personal fulfilment.

Magic Mouse Diet, n. Virtual weight loss achieved through the click of a mouse (digital alteration of a photo), rather than a reduction in calories. (Citation: Richard Woods, 'Does my digitally reduced bum look small in this?' *Sunday Times*, 12 January 2003.)

Manchurian Candidate, n. A media-friendly political candidate whose superficiality conceals the reality that he's a brainwashed drone, following the orders of a hidden master. Derives from the movie *The Manchurian Candidate*, originally starring Frank Sinatra, which tells the story of an American soldier who is captured, brainwashed, and programmed to become an assassin.

Meat Space, n. The offline world where people 'meet' as real, flesh-and-blood human beings.

Merkin, n. A pubic hair wig. Sometimes worn by exotic

dancers in order to appear fully naked while obeying local ordinances that require them to be partially clothed.

Milli Vanilli President, n. A president given speaking points via a wireless receiver hidden in his ear. Refers to the speculation that during the September 2004 presidential debate President Bush was wearing such a device. This rumour began when attentive TV watchers spotted a mysterious rectangular bulge between the president's shoulder blades, with wires running over his shoulder, beneath his suit. The bulge could have been a receiving device. Bush, however, insisted it was simply the result of his poorly fitted shirt bunching up. (Citation: Dave Lindorff, 'Bush's Mystery Bulge', *Salon.com*, 8 October 2004.)

MorF Internet shorthand for, 'Male or female?', a question often posed in online chat rooms when beginning a conversation. Asking the question does not guarantee a truthful answer.

Munchausen Syndrome by Internet, n. A psychological condition characterized by the telling of false tales of personal illness, specifically in an online setting. First identified by Dr Marc Feldman of the University of Alabama. Experts warn that an increasing number of participants in virtual health forums (online chat rooms or message boards) may be inventing problems to get attention.

Not Quite Human, adj. Said of those who have had too much plastic surgery.

One Per Cent Syndrome, n. The tendency of Americans to believe they're richer than they actually are, and to act accordingly. Based on a poll that revealed ten per cent of the American public consider themselves to be in the top one per cent income bracket.

Patina of the Real, n. The coarse, well-worn quality real things have, versus the overly smooth, processed look of fake stuff.

Payola Punditry, n. 'Independent' commentary paid for with bribes. What you get when media 'talking heads' accept money in exchange for secretly propagandizing for the government. Example: in early 2005 reporters for *USA Today* learned the Department of Education had paid conservative columnist Armstrong Williams $240,000 to 'say nice things about' the No Child Left Behind Act. Williams later insisted he believed everything he said about the Act, but he never bothered to tell his TV, radio, or print audiences about the financial arrangement.

Permanent Global Summertime, n. The ability of supermarkets to stock the same fruits and vegetables year round, as if it were always summer. With a global produce industry, fruits and vegetables are always in season somewhere.

Peter Panning, v. Using graphics software to attach an artificial shadow to an object. A common technique for adding the illusion of depth and realism to fake photos.

Pixel Plasticity, n. The ease with which the pixels that make up digital images can be altered and rearranged.

Ploughman's Lunch, n. A midday meal of cheese, pickles, bread, and salad served in British pubs. Marketed as a traditional farmer's meal, though it was created by the food industry in the 1970s. A faux traditional meal.

Used in the 1984 film *The Ploughman's Lunch* as a metaphor for the Thatcher administration's manipulation of the media.

Poop and Scoop, v. A stockmarket scam that involves swooping in to buy up shares after spreading negative rumours that cause a stock's price to depreciate; then selling at a profit once the rumours are discovered to be false and the price of the shares has recovered. The opposite of the pump and dump scam.

Post-mortem Divorce, n. A clause in a will stating that a husband and wife should not be buried next to each other. They may have pretended to tolerate each other in life, but they'll be damned if they'll spend eternity together.

Pseudo-event, n. An event staged purely for the purpose of generating publicity, as opposed to a real event that doesn't need press coverage to validate it. Examples include press conferences, celebrity interviews, and award ceremonies. Coined by Daniel Boorstin in his 1961 work *The Image: A Guide to Pseudo-Events in America*.

Pump and Dump, v. A stockmarket scam that involves hyping a stock in order to create buying interest and pump up the price, then dumping shares at a profit.

Quantum Bogodynamics, n. A theory of physics postulating that the universe contains objects of a bogus nature that infect surrounding areas with their bogusness. For instance, bosses often emit a high degree of bogusness, which explains why computers freeze, programmes fail, and presentations go awry at an unusually high frequency when they're around.

Realitician, n. Someone who freely distorts reality by telling people only what they want to hear, much like a politician.

Reality-Based Community, n. Those who prefer to view the world as it is, rather than how they'd like it to be. A play on the term 'faith-based community'.

Reality Distortion Field, n. A charismatic aura that allows some business people to warp how those in their presence perceive reality. Such power can be both motivational and delusional. Coined by Bud Tribble at Apple Computer to describe his boss, Steve Jobs, and still used most frequently in reference to Jobs.

Reality Index, n. The ratio of the time you spend in an unreal environment versus a real one. For instance, how much time you spend watching TV versus talking with friends. Coined by Kalle Lasn in *Culture Jam: The Uncooling of America*.

Real Person, n. Someone who is not an actor.

Real Reality, n. The opposite of virtual reality. The sometimes scary, increasingly unfamiliar world people enter into when they shut down their computer.

Renault Effect, n. The phoney shock and outrage expressed by officials when scandals they knew about (and may have been participating in) are uncovered. Named after the corrupt police chief in *Casablanca*, Louis Renault, who utters the classic line: 'I'm shocked, shocked to find that gambling is going on here', just before collecting his winnings. (Citation: Lucas Hanft, 'A Call to Avoid Casablanca-style Shock', *Yale Herald*, 26 April 2002).

RL, n. Internet shorthand for 'real life', as opposed to 'virtual life'. Example: 'I've decided to spend all my time online because RL sucks.'

Satirical Prophecy, n. A remark intended as a joke that later becomes true. Example: in 2004 the humour magazine *The Onion* spoofed the marketing efforts of razor-blade companies by satirically suggesting that Gillette was soon going to debut a five-blade razor with two lubricating strips. A year-and-a-half later, Gillette came out with a five-blade razor with two lubricating strips.

Scalpel Safari, n. A travel package that includes plastic surgery followed by a safari or a stay at a luxury resort. The idea is to get away for a few weeks and return home transformed and fully recovered, so that your friends and co-workers never have to see the ugly post-op healing process.

Silicone Challenge, n. A game in which players guess whether breasts are real or fake. Usually played with images of breasts found online.

Sim-ulated Reality, n. The exact replica of one's life and character that people tend to try to create when playing the video game *The Sims*.

Snob Hit, n. A boring movie or play that people pretend to like because they think they're supposed to like it.

Soundtrack Autism, n. The inability to know what emotions you're supposed to be feeling unless cued by a soundtrack.

Spinnish, n. The language of spin, spoken by people in public relations.

Spurious Rounding, v. Incorrectly rounding up bust and rib cage measurements when fitting women for bras. As a result of this common error, many women, according to experts, end up with poorly fitted bras. (Citation: Dr Matthew Wright, 'Graphical Analysis of Bra Size Calculation Procedures', *International Journal of Clothing, Science and Technology*, 2002; 14(1), 41–5.)

Subvertisement, n. An un-commercial. An advertisement created to subvert consumerism rather than promote it.

Surfer's Voice, n. The vacant, spaced-out tone of people browsing the web and conversing on the phone at the same time. Characterized by a high frequency of 'umms', 'errrs', and long pauses.

Surgiholic, n. A person addicted to plastic surgery.

Synthespian, n. A virtual actor created through digital animation. Examples include Buzz Lightyear from *Toy Story* and Gollum from *The Lord of The Rings*. In 2003 the MTV Movie Awards became the first show to reward the best 'virtual performance'.

Tanorexia, n. A syndrome in which the sufferer believes that no matter how tanned they are, they're not tanned enough.

Trout Pout, n. Lips excessively swollen due to cosmetic surgery (usually collagen injections).

Twinkie Defence, n. A criminal defence of temporary insanity due to eating too many Twinkies. More broadly, any far-fetched, bizarre argument offered by the defence in a criminal trial. Derives from the trial of Dan White for the 1978 murder of Harvey Milk. White's attorneys argued that their client should receive a reduced sentence because he was suffering from a temporary state of diminished mental capacity due to depression exacerbated by eating too many Twinkies. The jury agreed and sentenced him using only voluntary manslaughter guidelines.

Unread Bestseller, n. A book that many buy, but few actually read.

Vast Right-Wing Conspiracy, n. A supposed cabal of conservatives, working out of think tanks and foundations, that now controls much of the media and government. First used by First Lady Hillary Clinton in an interview on NBC's *Today Show* in January, 1998: 'For anybody willing to find it, and write about it, and explain it, is this vast right-wing conspiracy that has been conspiring against my husband since the day he announced for president. A few journalists have kind of caught on to it and explained it, but it has not yet been fully revealed to the American public.' Ironically, conservatives subsequently embraced the term.

Virtual Insertion, n. An object digitally inserted into a picture. For instance, fake billboards are often inserted into the background during the broadcast of sports games.

Virtual Reality, n. An artificial environment created by a computer. Coined in 1989 by Jaron Lanier, founder of VPL Research.

Voodoo Economics, n. Any economic theory based in fantasy, not reality. Coined by George H. W. Bush to describe the supply-side economic theory of his Republican rival, Ronald Reagan, who argued that the best way to stimulate the economy was to cut taxes for the wealthy since this would encourage them to invest and create jobs. Oddly enough, once Bush was chosen as Reagan's vice president, he became a firm believer in the voodoo economics he had once derided.

Where's the Beef?, int. A rhetorical question used to express the suspicion that something is all image and no substance. First used in a 1984 marketing campaign by the fast-food restaurant Wendy's. Entered mainstream usage the same year when presidential hopeful Walter Mondale asked this question of his Democratic rival Gary Hart.

Xenacate, v. To kill a TV or movie character off so completely that no chance remains of bringing her back from the dead, whether in a future episode or a sequel. Inspired by the TV show *Xena: Warrior Princess* (which was perhaps meant ironically since Xena herself often died and magically came back to life). Example: almost all of the red-shirted characters (except for Mr Scott) in the original Star Trek series were xenacated.

Yarase, n. A Japanese term for the staged events common on reality shows. Reality shows are particularly popular on Japanese TV, and are notorious for going to extremes of weirdness and cruelty that most American and European shows don't dare. Japanese fans of these programmes assume that the most shocking scenes are just *yarase*, which gives the fans an excuse for not being too disturbed by what they see.

Zen Spin, n. The public relations strategy of not spinning a story in order to appear more honest. A non-spin form of spin.

Zoomout Moment, n. When you suddenly see the big picture and realize you previously had no clue how things really are.

extracts reading groups
competitions books new
discounts extracts extracts
competitions extracts reading groups discounts
books new events reading groups extracts
events books discounts
new extracts books events
new titles reading groups
interviews reading groups
reading groups books extracts events new books
discounts events
new books events interviews books extracts
events new events
discounts extracts discounts books

www.panmacmillan.com

extracts events reading groups
competitions books extracts new books